Baby
Quilts

30 Full-Color

Patterns in Patchwork

and Appliqué,

Worked by Hand

and Machine Quilting

by Linda Denner

Photographs by Leonard Denner

Crown Trade Paperbacks
New York

This book is dedicated
to my parents, Grace and Herbert Groening.
They filled my childhood with love,
security, and happiness.

Acknowledgments

Special appreciation to Bobbie Brannin,
who offered her expertise in
quilting and English.

Published by Crown Publishers, Inc., 201 East 50th Street, New York, New
York 10022. Member of the Crown Publishing Group.
Random House, Inc. New York, Toronto, London, Sydney, Auckland

Crown Trade Paperbacks and colophon are trademarks of
Crown Publishers, Inc.

Book design by Linda Kocur

Pattern illustrations by Jennifer Harper

Manufactured in Hong Kong

Library of Congress Cataloging-in-Publication Data

Denner, Linda.
Baby quilts: 30 full-color patterns in patchwork and appliqué
worked by hand and machine quilting / by Linda Denner:
photography by Leonard Denner. — 1st ed.
1. Quilting—Patterns. 2. Patchwork—Patterns. 3. Appliqué—
Patterns. 4. Crib quilts. I. Title.
TT835.D453   1992   91-23821
746.9'7—dc20   CIP

ISBN 0-517-88006-7

10 9 8 7 6 5 4 3 2 1

First Edition

Contents

Glossary of General Directions

appliqué: In this technique a shape is cut from fabric and then stitched to a background material. For hand appliqué, mark the pattern lines on the right side of the appliqué fabric with a marking pen or pencil. Cut out the shape, adding a scant ¼″ seam allowance as you cut. The seam allowance will be basted under or turned under with your needle as you blindstitch the appliqué to the background fabric. The marking lines will be a guide when turning under the seam allowance.

For machine appliqué, the appliqués are cut without adding a seam allowance. The appliqué is then affixed to the background using a glue stick or fusible adhesive. (It is preferable to use a glue stick rather than white crafts glue or tacky glue because glue stick washes out easily and won't harden in the finished quilt.) Set your sewing machine for a satin stitch according to your instruction manual and stitch the appliqué to the background. It is advisable to position a stabilizer under your background layer, and tear it out once your satin stitching is completed. This will ensure unpuck-ered professional-quality stitches. For best results your thread color for hand or machine appliqué should match the color of your appliqué. Ordinary sewing thread should be used for hand appliqué. Machine appliqué can be enhanced by the use of embroidery thread in cotton, cotton/polyester, or rayon. Hand-quilting thread is inappropriate for use in appliqué.

backing: This is the bottom layer of your quilt. It is recommended that this be of a good-quality prewashed 100% cotton woven fabric. For machine or hand quilting select a busy print for this layer. Irregularities in machine and hand quilting will be concealed by a small print. A print fabric will show less wear. Additionally, this makes a more attractive presentation for a gift. Prewashed cotton flannel can also be a good backing for a baby quilt. Flannel is soft on baby and minimizes shifting in the crib.

bias: Fabric is woven on the loom with threads set in lengthwise and crossgrain directions. Di-agonally at a 45° angle to this weave, the threads are at their weakest point of construction. This configuration is referred to as the bias of the fabric. The bias of the weave has a great deal of stretch and elasticity. When patterns or strips are cut parallel to the bias they will reflect this stretch. The bias stretch is of advantage in bindings and appliqué.

basting: This is the method of sandwiching the three layers of your quilt—backing, batting, and quilt top—together. Tape the backing to a tabletop with masking tape, positioning the backing right side facing down. Lay the batting over the backing, smoothing it out. Finally, lay the quilt top over the batting, right side facing up. Smooth out all wrinkles. For hand quilting, pin the layers together with straight pins, working from the center of the quilt out. After all the layers are smooth and even, baste-stitch using a long needle or doll needle and a light-colored sewing thread. Secure the thread ends with a knot, and sew large stitches securely through all your layers, from the center to the outside edge of the quilt. Backstitch one stitch to end the thread along the outside edges. Repeat on the opposite end of your knot to make one horizontal thread line across your quilt. Continue this procedure every 3 to 4 inches, working horizontally only across the entire quilt. Diagonal basting threads will not successfully hold a quilt; they are appropriate only for a pillow top. If you stitch horizontal basting at 3″ intervals, you will not require additional stitching in a vertical grid pattern. Once your quilting is completed, the basting threads are all removed.

Basting a quilt in preparation for machine quilting is done in a somewhat different manner. Your layers are prepared as for hand quilting, but rather than thread basting you will use small safety pins to secure the three layers together. Brass safety pins size 00 to 1 are inserted and closed at approximately every 3 inches. This requires a great number of pins, as you may suspect. I usually use about 500 pins for an average-sized baby quilt. Using enough pins eliminates shift between layers. An advantage of safety pins is that the pins do not stab you as you quilt. Thread basting would not hold, and would be sewn in with your machine stitching.

batting: This is the inner layer that provides warmth for your quilt. Battings today are made from four materials: cotton, wool, polyester, and cotton/polyester in combination. The batting you select will be determined by your own preference and your climate. Wool bats are extremely warm, and easy to quilt. You can make beautifully small stitches with a wool bat; however, they are com-

paratively expensive and washing requires special handling. Cotton batting will necessitate quilting within each inch to prevent the batting from moving when washed. Cotton/polyester batting does not require close stitching but will need prewashing according to the manufacturer's instructions. Polyester batting is currently the most commonly used, and is available in a variety of weights, referred to as loft. Generally speaking, the higher the loft, the more difficulty in hand or machine quilting. All the quilts in this book were made using a low-loft polyester batting. This provides ease in quilting, and offers sufficient warmth when baby is provided with additional lightweight bedding. Low-loft batting is appropriate for both machine and hand quilting.

binding: This is a strip of fabric that is sewn to the outer edge of the quilt to finish the raw edges. The strips can be cut lengthwise along the grain of the fabric or on the bias of the fabric. The lengthwise grain is the most stable weave of the fabric. There is no movement or stretch with binding cut parallel to the selvage along the lengthwise grain. Lengthwise-cut binding is recommended for the edges of wall hangings. Curved edges require bias binding. The bias is cut at a 45° angle to the selvage edge of the fabric. Bias strips are stretchy, and will easily shape around curves.

In most cases, the quilt binding will be cut 1½″ wide. Join strips of bias by seaming their short edges until they are the length you require. Irregularities in cutting can be eliminated with pressing. Mark a ¼″ line along one

edge of a piece of cardboard. Press the strip, bringing one long raw edge over the cardboard to the ¼″ marked line. This will provide a sharp crease that can be used as a sewing guide. Inaccuracies along the outer edge will be pressed into this fold, and will not show in the finished project. Use only good-quality 100% cotton fabric for binding quilts.

Prepare the quilt edges by basting the top, batting, and backing together. Be careful to firmly draw these layers together within ¼″ of the outside edge of the quilt. Matching raw edges, pin the binding on the front side of the quilt. Set your sewing machine stitch length at 10 to 12 stitches to the inch. Use thread that matches the color of the binding. This is an appropriate time to use an evenfeed or walking foot on your sewing machine. This attachment eliminates shifting of the layers as you stitch. Sew the binding to the two long sides of your quilt first, sewing through all layers of the quilt. Trim any excess batting and backing that extends ¼″ beyond the outside raw edges of the quilt. Fold the outer raw edge of the binding even with the quilt raw edge. Fold the binding one more time and pin the binding to the quilt back even with the machine sewing line. Using a matching colored thread, blindstitch the binding to the quilt backing. After completing the binding attachment to the two long sides of the quilt, bind the top and bottom quilt edges. For these edges extend the binding at least ½″ beyond the outer quilt edge. This will allow you to fold under the short raw edges of the binding before hand-sewing the binding to the backing.

blindstitch: This stitch is sometimes referred to as an appliqué stitch. A right-handed person blindstitches from right to left; a left-handed stitcher sews from left to right. The needle, with a single strand of ordinary sewing thread, enters from the background and comes up and through the folded seam allowance edge of the appliqué. The needle then reenters the background fabric directly underneath and in line with the previously made stitch. The stitch travels to the next entry point on the wrong side of the background cloth and reenters the surface. Repeat the stitching sequence at intervals of no more than ⅛ inch. This stitch is preferred because little thread is on the surface to experience wear. For the least-visible stitch use ordinary sewing thread in color matching the appliqué.

Machine-sewn blindstitching can be a fast method of duplicating the look of hand appliqué. Refer to your owner's manual for specific settings. This stitch is a sequence of four or five straight stitches with one zigzag stitch that swings to the left of center needle position. To use this stitch in appliqué, shorten your stitch length to about 20 stitches per inch and shorten the zigzag swing, allowing your stitch to just bite the edge of your appliqué. Additionally, you can move your needle to the near left position if you have this capacity with your sewing machine. Use nylon monofilament thread in the top of your machine, and a sewing thread to match your background fabric in the bobbin. When you find it necessary to rip out stitches, remove the bobbin thread to release the seam. With a little practice, you can use this technique to

duplicate the look of hand appliqué in a fraction of the time. Several of the quilts in this book were constructed in this manner, and I think you would have great difficulty distinguishing the hand-blindstitched from the machine-blindstitched work.

block: This is a design unit in American patchwork. Most frequently blocks are square designs used as a single repeating unit or combined in multiples to create a patchwork surface.

borders: Borders are the outside bands that are sewn around the central quilt design. Borders can be constructed of single bands of fabric, multiple bands, or multiple patchwork units. To eliminate distortion and stretch, borders are best cut along the lengthwise grain of your fabric. If your border fabric requires piecing for sufficient length, seam the sections on the bias of the fabric. Bias piecing will conceal the seams.

fabric: Contemporary quilters have stretched our palette of quilting fabrics for wallhangings and wearable art. Since this book deals specifically with baby quilts, I would like to recommend 100% cotton fabric. Cotton is the most durable material and easiest to work with. Prewash your fabrics in cold water with a nondetergent soap made specifically for washing quilts. Iron the fabrics with a permanent press setting.

Color selection is very important with baby quilts. Keep your colors bright to attract baby's attention. Choose prints with a variety of scale: large, medium, and small. This provides interest in the surface design. Contrast is important, and your quilt should have

light, medium, and dark values. The most helpful suggestion when selecting fabric for any quilt is to stand the bolts up or drape fabric pieces upright on a vertical surface. Walk at least six feet away and judge how the fabrics work together from this distance. Quilters sometimes hold fabrics inches away and try to determine if one small motif is the same exact shade as in a coordinating fabric. This is utter nonsense. A quilt is viewed from across the room. The colors should work best from this distance, not under your nose. If you are timid about selecting colors, choose one important multicolor print for the quilt. Select all other fabrics to match and complement this print.

freezer paper appliqué: This is a method to mark and baste that assures the quilter of accurate appliqué pieces. Cut freezer paper sections the exact size of your appliqué templates. One side of the freezer paper has a waxed surface. Position this waxed surface face down on the wrong side of your appliqué fabric. Press this with a warm iron. Cut your appliqués a scant ¼″ seam allowance beyond the freezer paper edge. You can baste the excess seam allowance over the freezer paper, securing the basting stitches through the paper. Keep the fabric firmly up against the paper edges to maintain the shape of the pattern. Press and position the appliqué on the background fabric. Blindstitch the appliqué, minimizing the needle entering the paper. Stitch into the edge of the fabric whenever possible. When the appliqué is completely stitched to the background, remove your basting threads. On the wrong side of the appliqué, slash a small opening to insert your scissor tips. Trim away the excess background fabric under your appliqué, and leave ¼″ seam allowance under this appliqué of your background fabric. By placing a needle or fingertip under the freezer paper edge you can loosen the paper and pull it out.

There may be times when you use the freezer paper with the wrong side of the fabric against the unwaxed paper side. Fold the seam allowance over the waxed edge of the paper, pressing as you go. In many cases, this will fold under the excess seam allowance and thus serve as a substitute basting method. This works particularly well with curved edges such as a clam shell. Position the prepared appliqué on the background fabric, and press with a warm iron. The appliqué should adhere sufficiently to the background while you blindstitch it in place. Slash and remove the excess background fabric from behind the appliqué, and remove the paper through this opening.

grainline: This refers to the characteristics of the weave in woven cloth. The first threads that are positioned on the loom are threads that run lengthwise, or parallel to the fabric selvage. These are the strongest threads in the cloth and will not stretch or distort. Threads are then woven across the loom, perpendicular to the selvage. These threads are the crosswise threads of the fabric. Edges cut parallel to the crosswise grain will have a small amount of stretch. The grain that is at a 45° angle to the selvage is referred to as the bias. Bias edges run along the diagonal of the weave. Since the diagonal is the weakest point

of the weave, fabrics cut on the bias have a lot of stretch.

When bindings or fabrics from templates are cut it is important to keep in mind each grainline's characteristics. The side of templates parallel to the outside edge of the quilt should be placed on the fabric to be cut along its lengthwise grain to avoid stretching or distortion. Bindings made for a curved edge should be cut on the bias so they can stretch. Maintaining a straight edge is critical for wall hangings, so their bindings should be cut along the lengthwise grain of the fabric.

lattice strips: These are the bands that are sewn to the edges of each quilt block to frame and separate the blocks from each other or from other quilt design elements.

marking tools: Every day, new tools seem to be developed for marking fabrics and quilts. Textile experts caution us that some of the chemicals used in these pens may in time be hazardous to the fibers and shorten their lifespan. Baby quilts usually have a shorter life than most quilts anyway, because of their many washings. Using pens that permit a clear and accurate mark and following the manufacturer's directions, I have had no adverse experiences. In most cases, I prefer to mark my designs with a pencil with soft #3B or #5B lead. This lead permits very soft pressure, and will easily erase when necessary. For dark fabrics I use white pencil or a soap sliver. Do not use #2 school pencils as these will require too much pressure to make a mark, and will not erase.

Piecework patterns are generally marked on the wrong side

of the fabric. Position your template correctly on the grainlines on the wrong side of one layer of fabric. Use a sharp pencil to draw around this template. Templates for patchwork should include ¼″ seam allowance for ease in machine and hand piecing. In hand piecing, it is advisable to mark your ¼″ sewing line on the wrong side of your fabric with pencil. For machine piecing, use your sewing machine pressure foot or a marked line on the faceplate of your machine as a stitching guide.

Appliqués are usually marked on the right side of the fabric. This will serve as a guide when basting back the seam allowance. Appliqué templates do not contain seam allowance when employing this method. Mark the exact size and cut the appliqué, adding a scant ¼″ seam allowance. You will quickly learn to eyeball the correct amount.

mitering: Corners of two adjacent bordering fabrics are joined at right angles to each other, creating a mitered corner. When calculating yardage for this technique, it will be necessary to allow approximately ¼ yard more for a mitered border on a wall hanging or baby quilt. A full-size quilt will require ½ to ¾ yard more fabric. Cut your border strips along the lengthwise grain of the fabric in the width you require, including your ¼″ seam allowance on both sides. The length of the border should include the measurement of the side of your quilt with seam allowance, plus the width of the borders for the two outside corners, including their seam allowance. For example, if my quilt edge is 10½″, including seam allowance, and I am applying a 1″

border all around, I need to cut the border 10½" plus 1½" for one corner and 1½" for the second corner. The total measurement for this border length would be 13½". Each border should be marked with a ¼" seamline along the edge that will be attached to the quilt. The outside edge of the quilt should be marked with the ¼" seam allowance, as well. Match the sewing lines, and seam the border to the quilt on the marked lines, taking care not to stitch into the seam allowance at the corners. Attach two adjacent borders following this procedure. The border strips should overlap each other and extend the width of the borders at the corner. For marking, take the two short ends of the border and pin their outside short edges together. Working on the wrong side of the quilt, draw a line that will start at the precise corner of the quilt where the borders meet. This point will be connected to the outside point of the pinned border corners. This drawn line is the seamline that will create your mitered corner. Before sewing, check for accuracy by pinning along this line. Your seam should start at the quilt corner and continue to the border corner, creating a 45° angle seamline. When sewing, you should not take one stitch beyond the seamlines or the mitered corner will not lie flat.

While mitered corners require more attention than straight-sewn borders, the result is well worth the effort. Striped fabrics are ideal for mitering.

overlock stitching: This is a seam that combines a series of straight stitches to hold your cloth together with a wide zigzag stitch that swings to the right of the nee-

dle, encasing the raw edges. This stitch is offered commonly on modern sewing machines either as a built-in mechanism or by the addition of an attachment. This stitching is suitable for garment seams and eliminates fraying and excess bulk. Overlocking is accomplished most efficiently with an overlock or serger sewing machine.

piecing: This is the method of sewing two geometric shapes of patchwork together. Pin the raw edges together and match the sewing line of your two pieces. Use a single strand of ordinary sewing thread in a color that matches the darker of your two fabrics. Backstitch to begin your row of stitches. For hand piecing sew running stitches approximately ⅛" apart on the sewing line of your fabric. Backstitch to end your seam. Stay within your marked sewing lines on both sides when hand piecing.

Machine-piece using ordinary sewing thread in a color that matches the darker of the two fabrics you are joining together. Use a size 12 or 80 sewing machine needle in your machine for cotton-weight fabrics. Change the needle frequently, at least at the beginning of each project. In most cases when machine piecing it works best to assembly-line-sew units of piecework, one following another. Do not backstitch when piecing on the sewing machine. Most seams will intersect with another seamline, to secure them. Backstitching can prevent manipulating your fabrics for subsequent assembly techniques.

pressing: Quilting fabric should be pressed with a steam iron on the permanent press setting. Some

of the fabric dyes used today can melt and run on to adjacent fabrics when pressed with too hot an iron. It is advisable to press a block at the completion of its assembly. When you iron individual units as you go along, you often press small creases into the seams that will later be sewn into their construction. When the block is complete, press. Quilting seams are not pressed open, but are pressed flattened toward the darker-colored fabric. I usually press on the wrong side of the block, folding the seams in the direction I wish, and complete the operation by pressing the block on the right side. You want the bulk of the fabric in the seams to be pressed away from the center of the quilt. For this reason, a block that has seams constructed from the center out should have the seams pressed toward the outside of the block edge. Likewise, the border seams will lie best when they are pressed toward the outer edge.

When you are pressing a fabric that may not tolerate the heat of your iron, use a pressing cloth to protect its surface. Teflon pressing cloths are readily available for pressing fusible webbed fabrics, and for ironing delicate silks and lamé materials.

quilting: This is the process of stitching the three layers of your quilt together. Baste the layers, referring to the basting instructions above. For hand quilting, use quilting thread and a quilting needle. You may use a hoop or frame if you wish, but this is optional. Quilt with a running stitch through all the layers. Start stitching from the center of the quilt out toward the edges, to minimize uneven movement of the layers.

Use a single strand of thread no longer than 20 inches in length. You can put a single knot in the end to help anchor the thread. Enter the quilt through the top layer and snap the knot through the top surface, catching it in the batting layer. Bring your needle to the surface where you wish to begin your stitching. I take one backstitch at the beginning of my quilting line. This prevents the knot from popping out of the quilt layers. You will now begin to stitch. With a rocking motion, take running stitches through the layers. The spaces and the stitches should be even. With time and the gradual development of your eye-hand coordination your stitches will become small and even. When a thread is almost used up, reverse direction, traveling under the previously made stitches. This ending stitch falls between the thread layers and is not seen on the quilt back. Repeat this end stitching process until your completed stitches fail to move when you pull upon the threaded needle. Clip the thread flush with the surface of the quilt.

Geometric quilt patterns are traditionally stitched following the design shapes. Stitch ¼″ from your seams to avoid the bulk of your layers, or stitch "in the ditch," along the side of the seam that is free of seam allowance. Quilting patterns on appliqué quilts usually echo the outline of the appliqués. Somewhere between these two principles you will discover the fun and excitement of quilting your own way. As the photographs in this book show, I have employed all methods of quilting. Sometimes I ignore the surface design of the blocks and superimpose a 2-inch diamond grid over

the entire quilt surface. Variety is the spice of life. Enjoy yourself, experimenting creatively with your quilting. Today's polyester batting requires at least 5-inch spacing between your quilting lines to eliminate shifting when washing. The more quilting, the better!

Machine quilting has truly come into its own in the past decade. Perhaps this is the most appropriate method to use for baby quilts that are to be given happily away to as many little recipients as possible and go on to receive hard use. Baste the layers together as suggested for machine quilting. In most cases you will use nylon monofilament thread in the top of your sewing machine. Put ordinary sewing thread in the bobbin. The bobbin thread should match the fabric color of the backing. You should use either an evenfeed or a walking foot on your sewing machine for straight-line quilting or a darning foot for dropping the feed-dogs in freemotion quilting. In freemotion quilting the operator controls the direction and stitch length of the work. Refer to your owner's manual for machine settings. Select a good reference on machine quilting from your library or bookstore for the basic principles. Practice is the secret with machine quilting. Start with some unimportant small projects and allow yourself some time to build your skills. By the third project you will be ready to use this method on your best work.

reverse appliqué: This is a technique of hand appliqué in which the background fabric is marked and cut, with a scant ¼″ seam allowance added to the finished size. The seams are then turned under using a blindstitch.

As the background is turned under, a fabric layer is secured and positioned behind the cutout. The cutout may be a simple shape, such as a heart or leaf motif. This procedure can give the correct dimensional appearance to the appliqué picture, and is often easier to execute than ordinary appliqué. The background fabric serves as a window to reveal the underlayer of fabric.

rotary cutter: The introduction of the rotary cutter to quilting is similar to the development of the automatic washing machine. It is an essential tool for any quilter or craftsperson for the speed and accuracy it makes possible. The cutter is a circular razor set in a handle. It is used with a self-sealing surface or board. You will also need a thick plastic ruler that will display integers and angles. I prefer rulers that have yellow grid lines for ease in cutting dark fabrics. These also display ⅛-inch increments. The rotary cutter will cut accurately through more than four layers at a time. Cut strips, squares, borders, and every shape that has a straight edge with this tool. Replacement blades are readily available.

scissors: You will require at least three pairs of scissors for quilting. Purchase a good pair of shears for cutting large fabric sections and a small sharp pair of embroidery scissors for cutting out small appliqués. You should also have an inexpensive pair of scissors for cutting out your paper patterns and template plastic.

seam allowance: Piecing will use a consistent ¼″ seam allowance. Appliqué will require a scant ¼″ seam allowance.

setting triangles: These shapes are cut and used for the final assembly of the completed blocks into a quilt top. Grainline is an important consideration when cutting setting triangles. Determine the triangle's edge that will be parallel to the outside quilt edge and position the template with this outside edge along the lengthwise grain of the fabric. Keeping the outside edge of the triangle parallel to the lengthwise grainline of the fabric eliminates stretching and distortion of the finished quilt.

sewing machine: I am always challenged by nonsewers who piously state that real quilts are sewn totally by hand. I have been making quilts for almost twenty years, and I fail to see the merit of denying today's technology. I don't churn my own butter, or hand-piece a quilt. Machine sewing is faster and better than hand stitching in most cases. Get on speaking terms with your machine. Read the owner's manual. Keep your machine in proper running order. Today's modern machines make sewing a dream, and more fun than ever. The computers eliminate human error, and repeatable settings are as simple as flipping a switch.

strip piecing: This is the sewing together of similar- or varied-size strips of assorted fabrics to create a new fabric. The strips should be cut using a rotary cutter for accuracy. Machine-stitching the strips together is essential. Press the assembled fabric. Cut larger geometric shapes or appliqué units from this pieced fabric. This will add interest and variety to your quilt. Strip piecing is an excellent way of salvaging fabric odds and ends.

templates: These are the patterns made by placing template material such as sheet plastic over the patterns contained in this book or other sources. Templates for piecing should contain the seam allowance, while appliqué templates generally do not.

tracings: Lay tracing paper over the patterns in this book or other sources and trace them with a black indelible pen onto your paper. This will allow you to conveniently transfer the lines onto your fabric. One way to do this is to tape the tracing over a light source such as a light box or window. Position your fabric over the drawing and transfer the lines to your fabrics using a marking pen or pencil.

Introduction

This book is a collection of quilts designed for the baby or toddler. I have assembled designs suitable for the beginner to the advanced stitcher. With today's hectic schedules, projects that require months for completion are often left unfinished. With a full-time schedule outside the home as well as the traditional demands of family and community, quilters still long to create a special quilt for the newborn. Pride and creativity are the stitchers' driving force. Bearing this in mind, I offer many projects that will be quickly made, some in less than one day. By mastering the tools of today—a sewing machine, rotary cutter, and ruler—you can reduce the most involved designs to quick and easy projects. When time is not a consideration, and you are looking for a challenge, this book offers appliqué and pieced patterns to stretch your skills.

For those of you who enjoy creating your own "originals," my special chapter of "Mixed Blessings" will serve you well. The first chapter contains patterns that are made from traditional and original patchwork patterns. The second chapter presents appliqué designs. The appliqué patterns are presented whenever possible in full size. When the patterns were too large to present full size, we have provided the patterns at a reduced size, usually 50 percent (half size). When the pattern has been reduced at a percentage other than 50 percent, its finished size is indicated. Copy machines are available in libraries and printshops throughout our neighborhoods. Take the pattern to your local copy machine and enlarge the pattern to the measurement noted. This should eliminate the necessity of enlarging the design with a time-consuming grid method. The patterns of the first two chapters will work together in unlimited combinations to help you design your own quilts. This is demonstrated by my third chapter, entitled "Mixed Blessings." My favorite quilts combine appliqué and patchwork. In addition to the 10 designs included in this section, you will be able to select two, three, or more elements from the first two chapters, play with them, rearrange them, and create your very own original patterns. In this chapter as in the second chapter, guidelines are given for those patterns that have been reduced to fit on the page. My final quilt, Mixed Blessings, demonstrates the process that can be used to make hundreds of quilts.

The approximate time frame is noted on each pattern. Think of this notation more as a guide to how long an average quilter will take to complete a quilt. Time Frame 1 is a fast project, 2 will take several days, and 3 will take over a week. Remember that in art, less is more. Never underestimate the impact of a fast and simple classical design. If your fabric is wonderful, it will do the work for you and will be showcased best with a simple design. The Glossary in the front of this book explains and defines quilting terminology. If you are unfamiliar with a term or the method noted within the directions, refer to the Glossary for more detailed information.

I have one last suggestion before you begin your first quilt from this collection. As you thumb through the color photographs you may be struck by my selection of vibrant colors. Having taught quilting since 1977, I have been aware of the changes in popularity of colors and shades in quilting. More often than not, baby quilts are made in what I will refer to as "grandmother colors." These are soft pastels that look wonderful when photographed with wicker. These colors complement the furniture, but communicate little to the baby. Lately, some interior decorators suggest furnishing nurseries in black and white, since infants do not see color. Before I made my first quilt, I had two experiences that taught me very differently—Diana and Pam, my own daughters. Mothers and toy manufacturers know that baby is stimulated by strong, vibrant colors. Fortified with anger when I was told of the black-and-white theory, I did a little research to test my theory. According to psychologists, experiments show that two-month-old infants have color vision. Infants can discriminate a colored object from a white one, and will, indeed, prefer to look at the color. Infants can tell the difference between white, blue, greenish blue, orange, and red. Their color perception continues to progress, adding purple and other shades during their first six months until they can perceive the entire color palette. The lesson here, as today's educators will agree, is that stimulation is vital to a baby's development. Give babies something to look at! Make their environment suitable for their mental as well as their physical growth. Decorator trends come and go and are often fueled by promotion of new products. Our goal as quilters is constant: we make a quilt for beauty, warmth, and love. Translate that love by creating a bright rainbow of color to stimulate the brain and the heart of the new little owner.

o n e

Patchwork Quilts

When time and simplicity are important in the project you select, machine piecing is the answer. Review the owner's manual for your sewing machine if you have not used it in some time. Change the machine needle frequently, at least with the beginning of each new project. Piecing your quilt will utilize a size 80/12 needle. Machine quilting is done with a size 90/14 needle. Machine quilting creates a great deal of lint in your machine. Clean the lint with a brush and blow the excess out with canned air.

Patchwork will have ¼″ seam allowance. Check your presser foot to see if it is this wide. If it isn't, use a seam guide or masking tape positioned on the machine bed for reference. Take your time when you piece, pinning when necessary. Most errors are made when you rush, and when you have failed to keep the raw edges of your fabric pieces aligned. Rip your mistakes when necessary, reassuring yourself that all sewers rip. The more you sew, the more you rip. Don't live with a mistake; it will detract from your pleasure even if it is inconspicuous to others.

o n e

eyelet and lace

Time Frame 1

Finished size: 48″ × 54″

Materials required

*1¼ yards blue large-scale-pattern
calico print
1¼ yards peach calico print
1¼ yards small-scale calico print
1¼ yards cotton eyelet
1½ yards backing
½ yard binding
Baby-sized batting
6½ yards 3″-wide preruffled eyelet trim
Matching sewing and quilting threads*

■ **1.** Enlarge and trace pattern, and use this for hand piecing as a guide to check your measurements when following instructions below. This quilt is quickly made using a rotary cutter and speed sewing techniques.

■ **2.** Cut 3½″-wide strips lengthwise along the grain, parallel to the selvage, from each of your 3 calico prints. You will need one 45″-long strip and one 23″-long strip of each of these fabrics for the inside quilt design. Cut a corresponding number of 3½″-wide strips from your eyelet fabric. Do not use selvage.

■ **3.** Machine-sew an eyelet strip to each of the print strips, using ¼″ seam allowance. Before press-ing these units open, cut them into 3½″ segments.

■ **4.** Following the quilt photograph, arrange and assemble the horizontal rows of this quilt. The horizontal rows are made of 9 squares across. This quilt is made of 12 rows. Pin the horizontal rows together, carefully matching your seam lines, and sew them across with one seam.

■ **5.** Using the template, cut 20 squares of the print you will not be using for your border bands, and 16 squares from the outer-border calico. Assemble these units, combined with eyelet squares, into the corner nine patches.

■ **6.** Cut 2 strips of your first 2 print fabrics and 2 eyelet strips 3½″ × 36½″. Sew the bands together in groups of 3 strips with the eyelet positioned between your prints. Attach the bands to the long side of the quilt body. For the lower and top border bands cut 2 strips of each of the prints and 2 of the eyelet that are 3½″ wide by 27½″ in length. Sew these together. Sew the nine-patch corner segments to each short side of the top and lower border bands. Com-plete the quilt assembly by sewing these completed units to the top and bottom of your quilt top. Press.

■ **7.** Layer your quilt and baste. You can machine- or hand-quilt this project, referring to the Glossary for more detailed instructions.

■ **8.** When your quilting is completed, baste the outside edge of the quilt sandwich together. Sew preshirred eyelet trim to the right side of the quilt edge. The outer raw edge created from this assembly can be overlocked or bound with binding. Refer to the Glossary for binding directions.

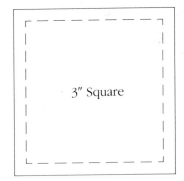

3″ Square

Seam Allowance Included

t w o

split rail fence

Time Frame 1

Finished size 32″ × 37″

Materials required

1 yard calico print for border
½ yard teal solid
½ yard green solid
¼ yard purple solid
¼ yard orange solid
1¼ yards backing
½ yard binding
Baby-sized batting
Matching sewing and quilting threads

■ **1.** This quilt is quick and easy to make using a rotary cutter and strip piecing on your sewing machine. All the strips used in the inner design will be cut cross-grain, perpendicular to the selvage of your fabric. The strips will be cut 2″ × 44″. Start by constructing the checkerboard section of the quilt block. Cut 4 strips of the purple and orange fabrics to be used in your checkerboard 2″ wide. Sew pairs of these strips together along their 44″ length, using a ¼″ seam allowance. Before pressing the bands open, cut across the sections at 2″ intervals. Press.

Sew 2 paired sections together to create a row of 4 squares. Press.

■ **2.** Cut 2 strips of each of the remaining 3 fabrics, the teal and green and the border print, cross-grain 2″ wide. Sew a band of these 3 fabrics. You will need to repeat this again to have sufficient units to complete all the blocks for the quilt. Press the sewn bands. Cut the bands into 6½″ segments.

■ **3.** Attach a checkerboard strip at the top edge of each of the banded segments. Start half of the checkerboard segments with an orange square, and the other half with a purple square. You should now have two sets of blocks, one starting with orange squares at the top left corner and the other starting with purple at the top left-hand corner.

■ **4.** Assemble the blocks into horizontal rows using the photograph as a guide. The checkerboard design will begin horizontally on the lower edge of your first row's block, followed by a block with the checkerboard on the right side of the block with the bands positioned vertically. Continue to alternate the blocks in this row till you have 4 across. The second row begins with the first block positioned vertically, checkerboard to the right side of the block. Alternate this with horizontal blocks to complete the row arrangement. Repeat these alternating row arrangements until your quilt has 5 rows across.

■ **5.** The borders are cut 4½″ wide on the lengthwise grain of your fabric. Sew the 2 long border sections on first. Trim and press. Complete the quilt top by sewing the border strips on the top and lower edges of your quilt.

■ **6.** Press. Layer your top, batting, and backing, then baste. Quilt by hand or machine.

■ **7.** When quilting is completed, baste the outside layers together firmly within ¼″ of the edge. Bind the quilt to finish the raw edges.

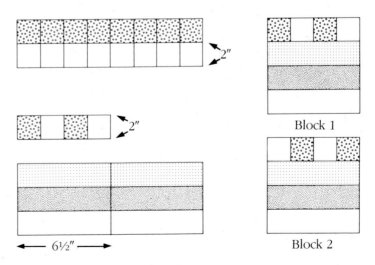

Block 1

Block 2

6½″

Seam Allowance Included

17

t h r e e

double irish chain

Time Frame 1

Finished size 36½″ × 56½″

Materials required

1 yard multicolored floral print
1 yard blue calico print
1 yard pink calico print
1½ yards backing
½ yard binding
Baby-sized batting
Matching sewing and quilting threads

■ **1.** This quilt is made using a strip-quilting method that is best executed with a rotary cutter. There are two blocks that are combined in an alternating pattern to create the design. All the strips for this quilt will be cut crossgrain, across the width of the calico, approximately 44″ wide. All the strips will be cut 2½″ wide. This includes your ¼″ seam allowance. If you select a striped fabric for this pattern, you can readjust the stripes into their upright position by turning the completed blocks one quarter turn.

■ **2.** Block 1 is made from three arrangements of strips. We will call the floral print fabric A, the blue print fabric B, and the background pink fabric C. You will need to cut 7 strips crossgrain from fabric A, 5 strips of fabric B, and 3 strips of fabric C to sew all the arrangements that will assemble block 1 for this quilt.

■ **3.** You will sew the strips together on the sewing machine down their long side, using ¼″ seam allowance. Sew the strips into the three sequences of row 1, row 2, and row 3 as illustrated. Once the strips have been constructed, press them. Using your rotary cutter, cut the sewn bands into 2½″ segments. Hold the ruler, which will serve as your guide, at a right angle to the outside edge of the band as you cut. This should help to keep your cutter straight. Cut all the bands into segments. You will need 16 cut segments of row 1 and of row 2, as these are repeated in each block. Row 3 does not repeat and will require only 8 segments.

■ **4.** Following the block diagram, sew your segments, which form the block's horizontal rows, into squares. Match at the seam intersections, and pin at these points to maintain accuracy. You will use 2 of row 1, 2 of row 2, and 1 of row 3 to create the block design. Press. This quilt requires 8 of block 1.

■ **5.** You are now ready to make block 2. Cut 2 strips crossgrain from fabric A, 2½″ × 44″. Cut a band from fabric C that is 6½″ × 44″. Sew the 2½″ strips to either side of the 6½″ strip. Press. Cut this band into 2½″-wide segments.

You will now cut 7 rectangles from fabric C that are 6½″ × 10½″. These measurements include ¼″ seam allowance. Sew the strips to either side of the rectangles to complete block 2. You will need 7 of block 2.

■ **6.** Alternating block 1 and block 2, sew the quilt into horizontal rows. Begin the first row, which has 3 blocks across, with a block 1 in the top left corner. The second row begins with a block 2. Continue to alternate these arrangements until you have 5 rows down. Sew the rows together to complete the assembly. Press.

■ **7.** The borders are cut 3½″ in width. The top and bottom borders are 30½″ × 3½″; the side borders are 50½″ × 3½″. The corner squares are 3½″. Sew the long side to the quilt first. Attach the squares to the sides of the short border strips, and seam these across the top and bottom to complete the assembly. Press.

■ **8.** Mark the quilting, and layer the backing, batting, and top together. Baste. Quilt by hand or machine. The outside raw edges should be bound to finish the project.

Patterns for this design are on the next page.

Double Irish Chain
(continued)

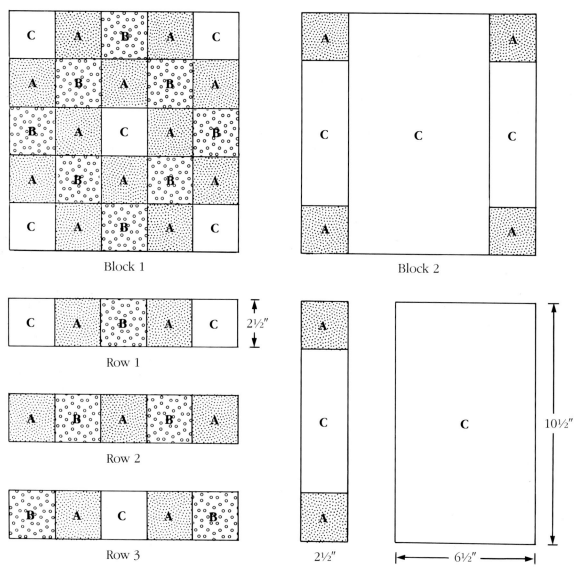

Block 1

Block 2

Row 1

2½″

Row 2

Row 3

2½″

C

10½″

6½″

Seam Allowance Included

sailboats

Time Frame 2

• • •

Finished size: 33½″ × 48½″

Materials required

1 yard royal blue solid
¼ yard yellow print for ships
¾ yard striped ticking for border
⅛ yard assortment of solids for sails
   and border squares
1¼ yards backing
½ yard binding
Baby-sized batting
Matching sewing and quilting threads

■ **1.** Begin by marking the triangle A template on the wrong side of your royal solid fabric. Each block will require 6 blue triangles; the entire quilt will require 36. From your assorted solids, mark 12 triangle A's. Using your yellow boat print, mark and cut 12 triangle A's.

■ **2.** Sew the triangle pairs together along their long side, carefully aligning their raw edges and sewing with an accurate ¼″ seam. Press.

■ **3.** Sew the triangle pairs into 2 rows each containing 2 pairs. Carefully position the assorted solids in the lower left corner of the squares. Press.

■ **4.** Using your rotary cutter, cut 2 rectangles that are 3½″ × 6½″ to be attached to either side of the sail section. Sew these and press. You can repeat this step for each of the sailboat blocks at this time.

■ **5.** Cut rectangle sections from your yellow print that are 3½″ × 6½″. Sew a yellow-print-triangle/royal-blue-triangle unit to either side of the yellow rectangle to make the boat section of the block. Repeat this for all the blocks at this time. Press them and sew them across the lower section of the sail segments you have previously assembled.

■ **6.** To complete the blocks, cut 2 strips crossgrain 3½″ in width from the royal solid fabric. Lay the lower edge of your blocks to this strip, and assembly-line-stitch them to this band. Cut the blocks even with their vertical edges to separate them from the band. This will complete the block by attaching the water section to it. Press.

■ **7.** When cutting the lattice from the striped ticking fabric you will want to maintain the stripe of your fabric. Cut 3 strips 3½″ by the fabric length for the vertical borders and 3 strips 3½″ crossgrain for the horizontal borders.

■ **8.** Using pattern B, cut 16 assorted triangles from your solids to make the setting squares. Assemble these as shown in setting square diagram.

■ **9.** Sew 3 rows of vertically striped lattice between 2 boat blocks. Use horizontally striped lattice between rows. Cut the horizontal lattice 3½″ × 27½″. Sew an accent square to the outside edge of each strip. Seam these bands between the block rows. Complete the quilt by seaming the top and lower borders across the quilt. Press.

■ **10.** Mark your quilting motif. Layer and baste the quilt for machine or hand quilting. Quilt the top completely before finishing your edges with binding.

Finished quilt and patterns for this design
are on the next two pages.

Sailboats

(continued)

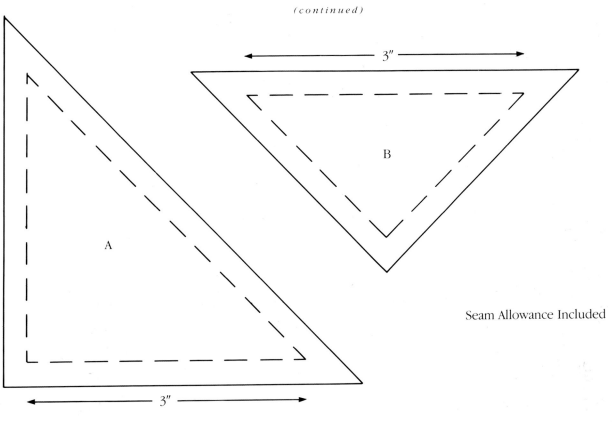

3"

A

B

3"

Seam Allowance Included

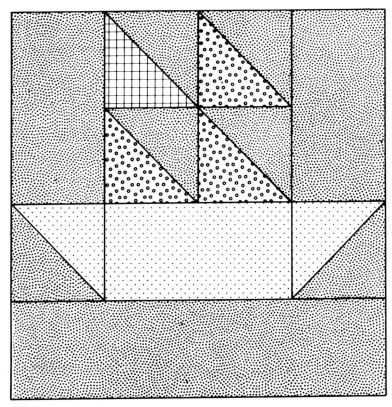

Block Diagram

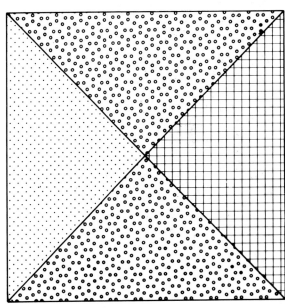

Setting Square Diagram

f i v e

nine patch and stars

Time Frame 2

Finished size: 44″ × 44″

Materials required

1¼ yards print for border and stars
¾ yard yellow print for background
¼ yard red solid
¼ yard green plaid with light
*   background for star blocks*
¼ yard white plaid with green
*   background for border*
1¼ yards backing
½ yard binding
Baby-sized batting
Matching sewing and quilting threads

■ **1.** This quilt is made of two alternating block designs. We will begin with the star block, which is best known as a Variable Star or Ohio Star. Using templates A and B, mark your fabric on the wrong side. Grainline is important in positioning the small triangular template. The long side of the triangle should be placed parallel to the lengthwise threads of your fabric, as indicated by the arrow. You will need 8 red triangles for each star, 4 green plaid, and 4 yellow background. Cut 4 yellow squares, and 1 red square per star using template B.

■ **2.** Assemble the star block, block 1, by first piecing the triangles together to make a square unit. Once these are sewn you are ready to stitch the star blocks together. Press.

■ **3.** Block 2, an extended nine patch, is best assembled by using our rotary-cutter/strip-piecing method. Cut 3 strips of yellow background crossgrain 1⅞″ wide by 44″. Cut 3 red solid strips the same size. Referring to the two combinations indicated in the diagram, machine-sew these strips together in units of 3, with ¼″ seam allowance. Press. Cut these units apart 1⅞″ in width to create the rows for the nine-patch mini-units used in block 2. Referring to the block diagram, piece the nine patches together. Press. Cut 4 yellow solid background squares using template B for each block 2. Complete this block by assembling the nine patches alternating with the solid squares. Press.

■ **4.** The quilt is assembled by sewing 2 rows of 3 blocks, beginning and ending with block 1, and sewing 1 block 2 in the middle.

The second row alternates this arrangement. Once the rows are sewn, stitch them together horizontally.

■ **5.** The first border is made of a 1½″ strip of green plaid that is sewn around the outside of the quilt. Press.

■ **6.** Cut the outside border along the lengthwise grain of your fabric to minimize stretch and distortion. The side borders are cut 3½″ × 36½″. They are sewn to the opposite sides of the quilt and pressed. The top and bottom borders are cut 3½″ × 44½″ and sewn to the quilt top to complete the assembly. Trim excess and press.

■ **7.** Prepare the quilt, batting, and backing to sandwich for quilting. Baste the quilt for hand or machine stitching. Once the quilt is completely quilted you will finish the raw edges with binding cut from the outer border fabric. The binding is cut 1½″ wide.

Patterns for this design are on the next page.

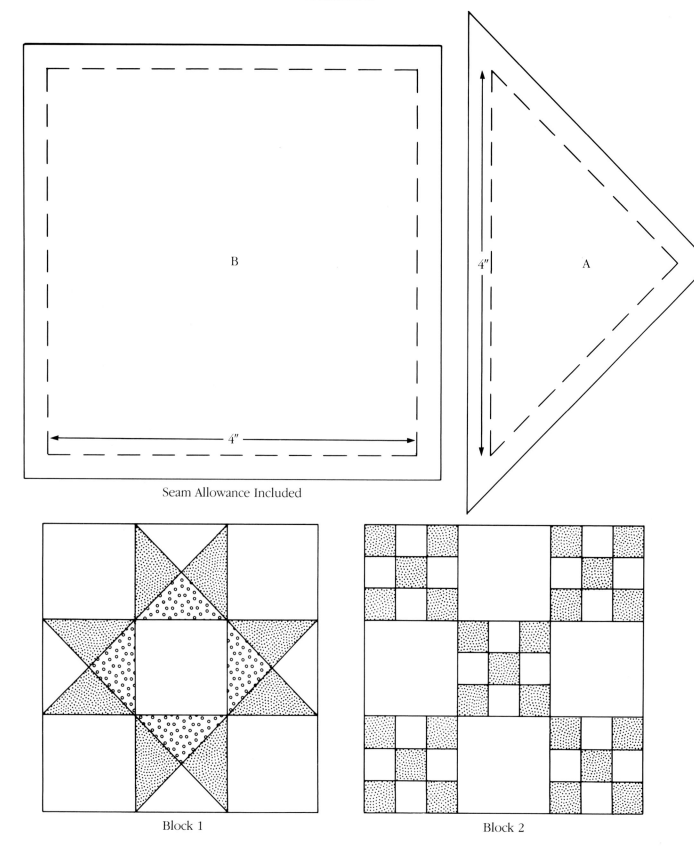

B

4"

Seam Allowance Included

4"

A

Block 1

Block 2

candy corn

Time Frame 2

Finished size 32½″ × 44½″

Materials required

*⅛ yard each of at least 10 solid or
print calicos for the large
triangles, template A*
*1½ yards pink print background fabric
for template B and borders*
½ yard binding
1⅓ yards backing
Baby-sized batting
Matching sewing and quilting threads

■ **1.** Enlarge and trace templates A and B. This quilt is made using approximately 77 units commonly known as Flying Geese. They are made by cutting 77 template A triangles from an assortment of fabrics, and 154 small triangle B's from your background fabric. Sew 1 small triangle to the left short side of your large triangle, open, and press. Complete the unit assembly by sewing a second small triangle to the right short side of the triangle and pressing. Sew these units into rows. Referring to the row assembly diagram, sew the first diagonal row with 5 flying geese. The second row uses 12 flying geese, the third 19, the fourth

20, the fifth 14, and the sixth and final row 7.

■ **2.** When you have completed the flying geese rows it is time to begin assembling the quilt. Cut 2 corner triangles using enlarged template C. The bands between the rows will be cut 3½″ wide. In order to maintain the grainline in this quilt it will be necessary to cut these bands on the bias of the fabric. To start cutting, position your template C on the bottom right corner of your fabric. Mark the hypotenuse, or diagonal, of the triangle on your fabric. Lay one long side of your ruler on this marked line and measure strips 3½″ apart that will maintain this angle. These strips will be pieced together to create the alternate bands.

■ **3.** Begin the quilt assembly by sewing a corner triangle to a row of 5 flying geese. It will be necessary to stitch template C to the beginning and end of your flying geese rows to set them in a diagonal direction. Sew their long sides parallel to the outside quilt edge as shown in row assembly diagram. Sew a band to the first

row, and attach your next row of patchwork. Continue to alternate rows with bands until you complete the rectangular quilt with a final corner triangle. Press.

■ **4.** The outer border is cut 4½″ in width parallel to the lengthwise grain of the fabric. This is necessary to eliminate stretch. The side borders are cut and attached first. These are 4½″ × 36½″. The two remaining borders are 4½″ × 32½″. Sew and press these to complete your assembly.

■ **5.** Prepare your backing and batting to sandwich the quilt. Baste the layers together for hand or machine quilting. Quilt the entire top before binding. I quilted the border by continuing the flying geese linear design motif into the border fabric. This was a simple quilting pattern. Extend the row lines with a marker.

■ **6.** Bind the quilt with 1½″ strips to complete this project.

*Finished quilt and patterns for this design
are on the next two pages.*

(continued)

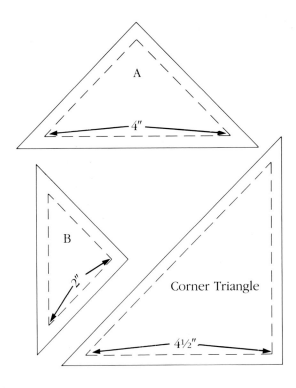

A

4″

B

2″

Corner Triangle

4½″

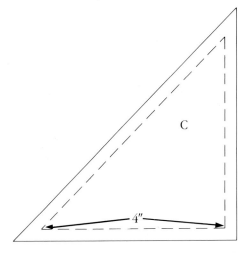

C

4″

Half-Size Patterns

Seam Allowance Included

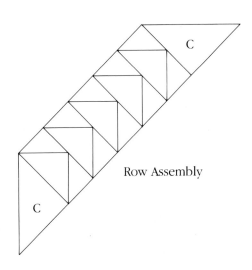

C

Row Assembly

C

pinwheel scraps

Time Frame 3

Finished size: 33½″ × 41½″

Materials required

*½ yard assorted yellow prints that
have light and dark value
differences*
*½ yard assorted lavender/purple prints
that have light and dark value
differences*
*½ yard assorted teal to aqua prints
that also differ in value*
*½ yard assorted pink prints that also
differ in value*
*1 yard light-blue print for border and
setting triangles*
*½ yard medium-blue print for setting
triangles and striped border*
1¼ yards backing
Baby-sized batting
Matching sewing and quilting threads

■ **1.** Enlarge and trace template A and cut 8 for each block in this quilt. The block is commonly known as a Pinwheel. Following the block diagram, piece the triangles together to make squares, then seam them into 2 rows. Maintain the value color placement as indicated. You will need 5 whole blocks and 2 half blocks of yellow for the first quilt row. You will need 6 purple blocks, 5 aqua-teal blocks with 2 half blocks, and 6 pink blocks for the final row. Press the blocks once they are assembled.

■ **2.** Enlarge and trace templates B and C for the quilt setting, as described in the Glossary. You will cut 11 of template B from the medium-blue, and 33 of this tem-

plate from the light-blue print. Keep the long side of template B parallel with the lengthwise grain of your fabric when cutting. This will prevent the outside edges of your rows from stretching. Using template C, cut 6 pieces from the light-blue print and 2 from your medium-blue print.

■ **3.** Refer to the placement diagram to assemble your quilt into rows. The rows for this quilt are placed in what is commonly referred to as a zigzag setting. The blocks are sewn into vertical rows. Begin by sewing a medium-blue triangle B to the left side of a pink block, and a light-blue triangle B to the opposite side of this block. Sew the triangles' short sides to the block, keeping the long edge free as the outside edge of the row. Continue in this manner for 6 pink blocks. Referring to the diagram, complete the row by adding a small triangle C in the appropriate color.

■ **4.** Use the placement diagram to complete the quilt block assembly. Press.

■ **5.** The first border of this quilt is strip-pieced. Assemble 1″ strips of the medium-blue print and 1½″ bands from scrap pieces randomly selected from your leftover prints. The border width is 2½″ and should be assembled to match the outside lengths of your quilt. You will need two 1½″ × 21½″ bands and two 1½″ × 33½″ bands.

■ **6.** Cut the outside border bands

lengthwise along the grain of your fabric, parallel to the selvage. This will stabilize the outside edges of the quilt. The 2 long side borders are cut 4½″ × 34½″. Sew and press these to the quilt sides. The 2 remaining border sides are cut 4½″ × 33½″. Sew and press these borders to complete the quilt top.

■ **7.** Baste the quilt in preparation for machine or hand quilting.

■ **8.** When the quilting is completed, you are ready to bind the edges. The binding of this quilt is made from the assorted scraps left over from the blocks and border. This is in harmony with the design. Take care to cut the strips lengthwise along the grain even when they are cut from scraps. You can readily determine the grain by gently pulling along the weave of the fabric. The side that is parallel with the lengthwise grain will not stretch or show movement. Cut a length 4½″. The width of this binding will be a standard 1½″. Assemble lengths that will equal that of the quilt edge. If you are short in some direction, make your final strip 5″ to 5½″ in length to allow for the variation. This will not be a discernible change to the viewer's eye. Press the binding seams flat before attaching to the edges of the quilt. Attach this binding as described in the Glossary.

*Patterns for this design are shown on
the next page.*

Pinwheel Scraps

(continued)

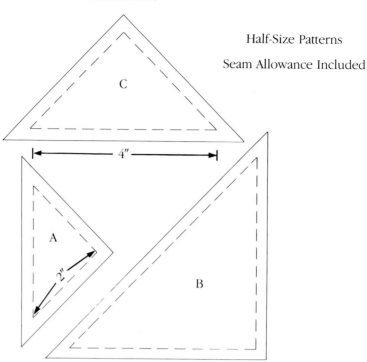

Half-Size Patterns

Seam Allowance Included

For 3⅜ squares (A)
cut (B) 5⅞-6" and
(C) 4⅜-4½"

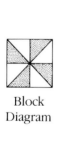

Block
Diagram

Placement Diagram

ribbons for the baby

Time Frame 2

Finished size: 32″ × 42″

Materials required

1½ yards muslin
½ yard teal print for first border and
*   block frame*
12 assorted ⅛-yard pieces of
*   coordinating calico prints and*
*   solids for the ribbon blocks*
1¼ yards backing
Baby-sized batting
Matching sewing and quilting threads

■ **1.** Trace templates onto plastic or other appropriate template material. Using triangle template A, mark and cut 12 triangles from your main ribbon color, 6 from the coordinating ribbon color that represents the underside of the bow, and 18 from the muslin. Please refer to the diagram for clarification. Using square template B, mark and cut 6 main color pieces, 4 coordinating print pieces, and 12 muslin pieces. Shapes C and D can be cut using your rotary cutter and ruler. Shape C is 2½″ × 1½″. Each block will use 4 C rectangles. Shape D is 1½″ × 5½″. These templates are given with the ¼″ seam allowance.

■ **2.** The first step in assembling this block is to sew each printed triangle to a muslin triangle. Seam along their diagonal side using ¼″ seam allowance. Press.

■ **3.** Begin construction of this block by assembling the top bow units. Refer to the completed block diagram. The top left- and right-hand units are identical except that the second-row square and triangle are reversed. Press. The muslin is the background color.

■ **4.** Sew an accent-colored square to the lower end of a C strip, and sew a bow unit to either side of this to finish the top half of the ribbon block.

■ **5.** Refer to the diagram to assemble the remainder of the block. Sew the 2 block sections together to complete 1 block. Press.

■ **6.** Your quilt will require 6 blocks of this design. The block's completed size should be 7½″ square.

■ **7.** When you have all 6 blocks completed, it is time to frame them with a unifying band of color. Cut 1½″-wide strips from the length of your first border fabric. Piece these strips together whenever you require greater length. Piecing the band diagonally on the bias will keep the seaming inconspicuous. Press. Sew these bands in an assembly-line manner around all 4 sides of each of your blocks.

■ **8.** From the muslin, cut 3″ bands for the lattice strips of the quilt. Cut these lengthwise along the grain. Sew 2 blocks together horizontally by attaching 3″ strips of muslin that has been cut 9½″, the height of your framed blocks. Sew a 3″ × 9½″ strip to either edge of the blocks to make your row across. Repeat this for the second and third quilt rows.

Using a 3″ band cut 21″ in length, set the rows together. Sew a 3″ × 21″ strip to the top and lower edges of the quilt. Press.

■ **9.** Cut 1½″-wide strips and assemble the required length of this from your border/framing print. Sew this band around all the outer edges of the quilt.

■ **10.** The outer border is cut 3″ wide by the length of your muslin. Cutting these strips lengthwise will stabilize your edges. Sew this band to the long sides of the quilt and then to the top and lower edges to complete your quilt top. Press.

■ **11.** Layer the quilt with batting and backing. Baste for machine or hand quilting. Quilt the entire top before you bind the edges of your quilt. Binding will be made using the muslin fabric, cut on the bias, and should be 1½″ wide.

Finished quilt and patterns for this design are on the next two pages.

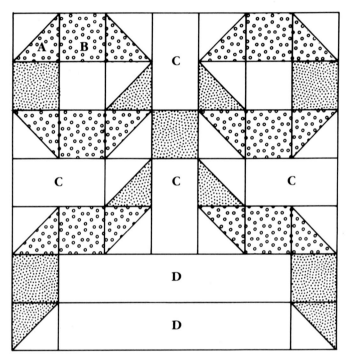

Diagram Shown Half Size

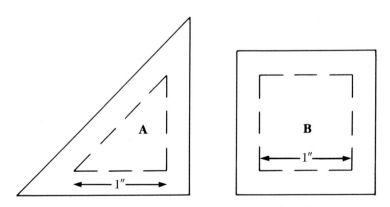

Seam Allowance Included

pieced stars

Time Frame 3

. . .

Finished size: 40″ × 59″

Materials required

1½ yards muslin
¾ yard each of red, blue, and green
  prints
1½ yards backing
1 yard green print for binding
Baby-sized batting
Matching sewing and quilting threads

■ **1.** Enlarge and trace templates for both size stars from patterns given. Templates A, B, and C are for a 12″ eight-pointed star, and D, E, and F will make a 3″ eight-pointed star. Mark your fabric with an accurate cutting line, and you will find it helpful to mark a line ¼″ within your cutting line to use as a seam guide. Lay the template on your fabric with the arrow parallel to the lengthwise grain.

■ **2.** When assembling an eight-pointed star there is a recommended order to follow. Begin by accurately lining up the sewing lines of two diamonds. Stitch by hand or machine; however, do not sew past your marked sewing line. When hand piecing, backstitch to end your seam. Sew all your diamonds into 4 pairs. Carefully matching your sewing lines again, sew 2 pairs to each other to make half the star. Repeat this with the other half. Now you are ready to seam the 2 halves together. Pin and match your center seamlines and stitch on the sewing lines only. When hand piecing it will be helpful to sew through your seam

allowance, passing your needle through the seam. This makes pressing the star easier.

When the star is assembled, you are ready to insert your corner squares and triangles. Mark an accurate sewing line ¼″ from the cutting line as you did for the diamonds. The seams to insert these shapes will meet your diamonds at right angles. It is recommended to seam with a two-step procedure. Pin the edges together, taking care to match seam allowances. Sew the seam from the inside corner of the star toward the outside edge. Repeat this procedure with the other side of this shape, stitching from the inside to the outer edge. You will sew all the squares and triangles, following the block diagram to complete the star blocks. Press the blocks after assembling.

This quilt will use six 12″ star blocks and eight 3″ star blocks.

■ **3.** Cut 3½″ strips from the length of your muslin for the border. Sew a 3½″ × 12½″ strip to either side of the large star blocks and repeat for rows of large star blocks. Assemble 2 small star bands between the block rows. Cut two 3½″ × 42½″ border bands from muslin. Sew these to the long sides of your quilt top. Cut 4 more muslin bands that are 12½″ × 3½″. These will form the top and lower lattices. Sew 3 small stars, alternating with 2 muslin bands for top and bottom bands.

Sew the assembled bands to the quilt.

■ **4.** You are now ready to make our Seminole pieced outer border. This is a strip-pieced method creating an intricately pieced border in a short time. You will begin by cutting a 1½″ × 44″ strip from each of your 3 colored fabrics, and 9 strips 1½″ × 44″ from your muslin. You will sew these together in bands of 3 with muslin strips on the outside. Sew a muslin band to either side of the red strip for unit A, a muslin band to either side of the blue for unit B, and a muslin band to either side of the green for unit C. Press the 3 units. Cut the units into segments that are 1½″ wide. Refer to the piecing chart, and assemble these segments as shown, staggering segments and matching a print square to a muslin square. The segments are constructed by repeating your three color combinations in sequence: ABC, ABC, ABC, and so on. Cut and strip as many of these units as will be sufficient in length to attach to your quilt sides. You will need 2 bands that are 54½″ in length and 2 short ends that are 35½″ in length.

■ **5.** Before sewing the Seminole border to the quilt it will be necessary to sew a 1½″ band of muslin to the outer quilt edge. This will separate the border and create the illusion of floating small squares. Sew this band to the quilt. With a ruler, draw a line on the wrong side of your completed Seminole bands that will be your sewing line. This line should touch the top corner of each colored square in your Seminole band. Lay your band over the quilt edge and stitch on this marked line. It is not necessary to trim the points off your triangle edges before stitching. After your seam is completed you can trim the points using your rotary cutter. It will be necessary to trim away some of the squares at the corner of each side to miter the corners. Refer to instructions in the Glossary.

■ **6.** The quilt has a final outside border of muslin. Cut 1½"-wide strips lengthwise along the grain of your fabric. Sew these to the long sides of the quilt, and repeat by adding strips to the top and bottom as well. Press.

■ **7.** Layer your quilt top for basting. Machine- or hand-quilt. The raw edges are completed with binding made from the green print when the top is completely quilted.

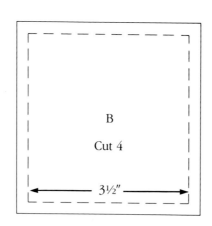

B

Cut 4

◄――― 3½" ―――►

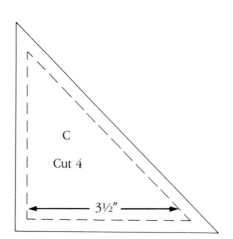

C

Cut 4

◄――― 3½" ―――►

Seam Allowance Included

Half-Size Patterns

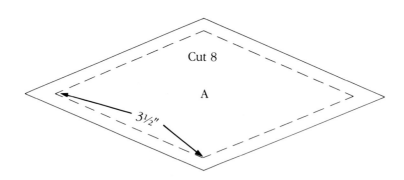

Cut 8

A

3½"

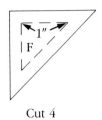

Cut 4

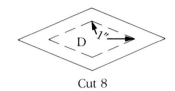

Cut 8

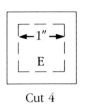

Cut 4

Half-Size Patterns

Seam Allowance Included

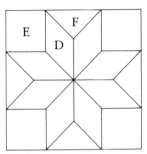

Block Diagram

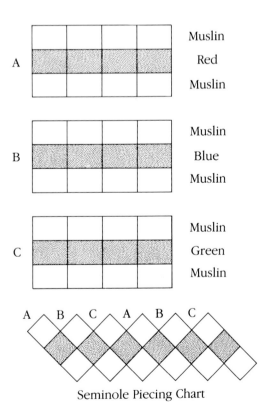

A   Muslin

Red

Muslin

B   Muslin

Blue

Muslin

C   Muslin

Green

Muslin

A   B   C   A   B   C

Seminole Piecing Chart

t e n

baby's first step

Time Frame 3

Finished size: 44″ × 56″

Materials required

1 yard light multicolored print for background
1 yard green calico for blocks and border
½ yard yellow print
1 yard peach print
¾ yard lavender solid for triangles and binding
1⅝ yards backing
Baby-sized batting
Matching sewing and quilting threads

This quilt is made of 2 blocks. The construction of the blocks is best accomplished with the use of a rotary cutter and by machine piecing. The quilt is made in half sections. Refer to half quilt layout.

■ **1.** For block 1 cut strips from 4 of your fabrics, 2″ wide by 44″ long. Cut 2 strips from each of the background print, peach, yellow, and green fabrics. For strip pair 1 sew a strip of yellow and a strip of green together along their 44″ length using a standard ¼″ seam allowance. For strip pair 2 sew strips of peach and yellow together in the same manner. Cut these bands into 2″-wide segments. Your quilt will require 24 of block 1. Save time by sewing your first 2 strip pairs into four-patch units as diagrammed. Sew 48 four-patch units together. Press.

■ **2.** Cut additional strips 2″ × 44″ from the background, green, yellow, and peach prints. Assemble strip pair 3 from the background and green prints, and strip pair 4 from the background and peach prints, referring to diagrams. Cut these pairs into 2″ sections. In an assembly-line manner, sew a 2″-wide green strip along the 3½″ side of cut segments from strip pair 3 to form unit A. Sew a 2″ peach strip along the 3½″ cut segments from strip pair 4 to form unit B. The quilt will require 24 each of unit A and unit B. To assemble block 1, refer to the block diagram, and sew a unit B to the right side of a four-patch unit for the top half of the block. Sew a unit A to the left side of a four-patch unit to assemble the lower block half. Sew the 2 halves together to complete the block assembly. Press.

■ **3.** For block 2, trace triangle template A from the Sailboats quilt pattern, page 23. Cut 96 triangles from your background fabric, and 96 from your solid lavender. Sew these together along their long sides using ¼″ seam allowance. Press. The four-patch unit used in combination with the triangles to make block 2 is cut from your background fabric and your peach print. Cut three 2″ × 44″ strips from each of these fabrics. Sew a background and peach strip to-gether along the 44″ length by ma-chine using a standard ¼″ seam allowance. Press and cut these into 2″ segments. Sew these into four-patch units, reversing the order on their second row to create a small checkerboard. Refer to the block diagram, and sew 2 triangles and 2 four patches together to complete the block. Press.

■ **4.** You are now ready to sew the quilt together. Follow the half quilt layout and assemble the 2 quilt halves. Join the 2 halves with a seam in the center. Refer to pho-tograph for assembled top.

■ **5.** Cut 2″-wide strips lengthwise along the grain of your back-ground fabric for the first border. Sew these together, attaching the strips for sufficient length. Sew to the top and lower edges, and com-plete this border by sewing the strips to the long sides of the quilt. The outside border is cut 3½″ lengthwise from your green print. Cut and piece as necessary. Sew to the outer edge in the same man-ner as the first border. Press.

■ **6.** Layer the quilt with the bat-ting and backing and baste for hand or machine quilting. Quilt the entire quilt top before finish-ing the outside edge with laven-der solid binding.

Patterns for this design are on the next page.

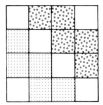

Block 1

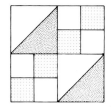

Block 2

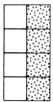

Strip
Pair 1

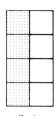

Strip
Pair 2

Strip
Pair 3

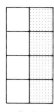

Strip
Pair 4

Four-Patch
Unit

Unit A

Unit B

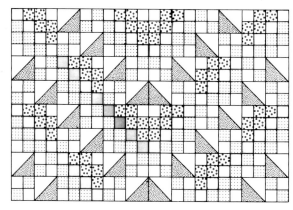

Center Seam

Half Quilt Layout

t w o

Appliquéd Quilts

Through appliqué the quilter represents line drawings with fabric and stitchery. If you have despaired of matching seamlines and seaming perfect triangles, appliqué offers an alternative. When time is limited and your sewing machine offers a satin stitch, consider executing these patterns by machine. Follow the suggestions for each method in the Glossary.

The designs in this book, save one, are my own. Lillian Baglivi of Long Island, New York, a dear and talented quilting friend, designed Country Hearts, featured in this chapter. Since it was a favorite of our quilting club members, I knew it would be a great addition to this book.

twinkling stars

Time Frame 1

Finished size: 27½″ × 33½″

Materials required

¾ yard white solid or print for background
⅞ yard printed stripe for outer border
12 assorted 6½″ scraps of solids or prints with primary colors
¾ yard backing
½ yard solid for binding
Baby-sized batting
Matching sewing and quilting threads

■ **1.** Cut a white background measuring 20½″ × 26½″. Mark ¼″ seam allowance parallel to the outside edge. Mark 1″ away from this line, on the right side of your fabric. This creates a rectangle that measures 18″ × 24″ on your white background. Divide this rectangle into three 6″ boxes across and four 6″ boxes down. The marked rectangular grid lines will be your quilting lines.

■ **2.** Enlarge and transfer the star pattern to template material. For machine appliqué, use a fusible webbing to position the appliqués to your background fabric. Do not add seam allowance for machine appliqué. For hand appliqué, mark the star on the right side of your fabric and cut the fabric add-ing a scant ¼″ seam allowance. Turn the excess seam allowance under with your needle as you appliqué the stars to the background with a blindstitch. Trim away excess seam allowance, tapering into the points to achieve sharp angles. At the converging star corners, clip up to the marked line.

■ **3.** Cut 4 border bands 34″ × 3½″ from striped fabric. Sew the border to the outer edge of the four sides of the white background. Do not stitch into your ¼″ seam allowance. Miter the corners to achieve a framing effect, according to instructions in the Glossary. Press.

■ **4.** Layer the top, batting, and backing. Baste for machine or hand quilting. Quilt around the stars and on the marked lines of your background fabric. Quilting between the lines of the striped border creates the illusion of a strip-pieced border.

■ **5.** Bind the raw edges with 1½″ binding to complete the quilt.

Half-Size Pattern
Seam Allowance Not Included

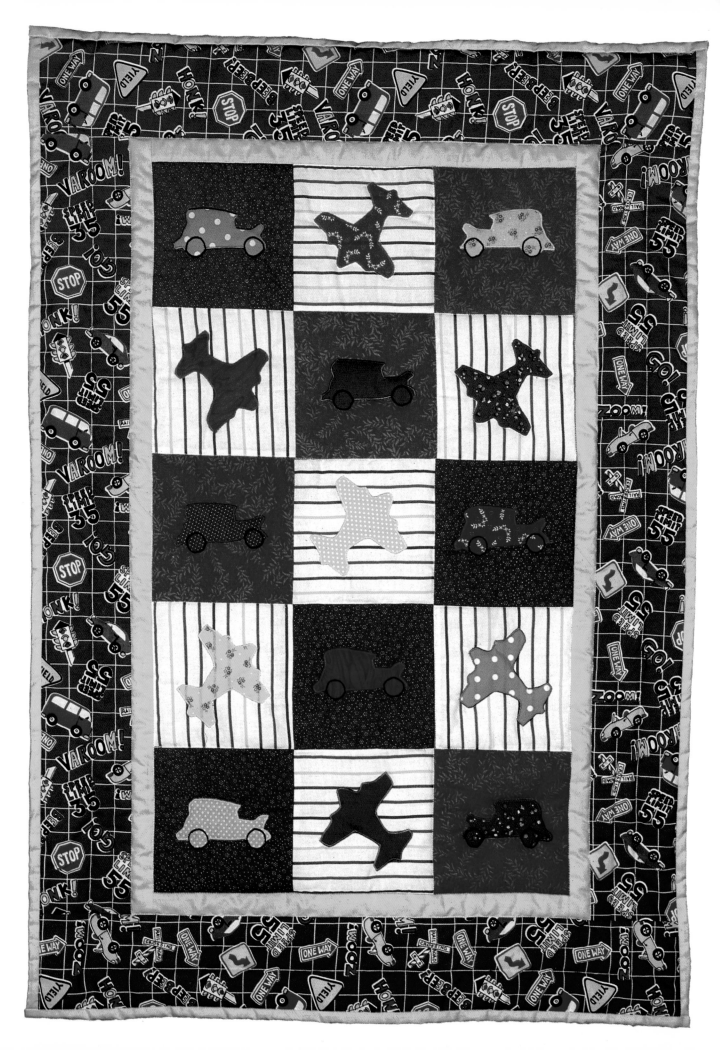

t w o

cars and planes

Time Frame 1

Finished size: 28½″ × 40½″

Materials required

*¼ yard each of bright red, blue, and
   green prints or solids
½ yard white print
1 yard yellow solid for border,
   appliqué, and binding
1 yard border print
1¼ yards backing
Baby-sized batting
Matching sewing and quilting threads*

■ **1.** Cut fifteen 6½″ background squares: 4 blue, 7 white, and 4 red. Sew the squares together 3 squares across and 5 rows down. Arrange the colors as illustrated in photograph. Press.

■ **2.** Enlarge and transfer the car and airplane patterns to template material. Mark the appliqué fabric on the right side of the fabric for hand appliqué, adding a scant ¼″ seam allowance as you cut. For machine appliqué use a fusible adhesive, following the manufacturer's directions. Refer to the photograph for appliqué placement.

■ **3.** For the first yellow border cut 2 strips 18½″ × 1½″ and 2 that are 32½″ × 1½″. Sew the top and bottom bands on first and complete the framing with the side bands. Press.

■ **4.** Cut the outside borders along the lengthwise grain of your border print. You will need 2 strips 32½″ × 4½″ and 2 strips 28½″ × 4½″. Sew the long side strips on first, and complete the assembly by attaching the top and lower borders. Press.

■ **5.** Layer the quilt top, batting, and backing. Baste for hand or machine quilting. Quilt by stitching around the appliqués and "in the ditch" following the outline of the squares and border seams.

■ **6.** When the quilting is completed, bind the raw edges using 1½″ binding cut from the yellow fabric.

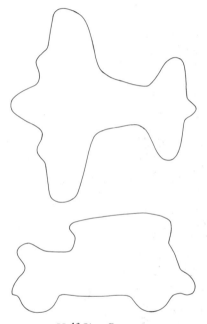

Half-Size Patterns

Seam Allowance Not Included

t h r e e

egg tree

Time Frame 2

・　・　・

Finished size: 24½″ × 32″

Materials required

23½″ × 17½″ blue solid for background
¾ yard striped print for border
½ yard turquoise print for binding and first border
12 assorted 4″ print squares for egg appliqués
6″ square white print or solid for bunny appliqué
¼ yard white piqué for tree
4 assorted 1½″ × 6″ strips for flowerpot
⅛ yard pink for heart appliqués
Ribbon floss
½ yard ½″-wide pastel-colored satin ribbon
7″ lace trim
Pom-pom
Embroidery floss for bunny face
½ yard polyester batting
Matching sewing and quilting threads
¾ yard backing

■ **1.** Center-crease your background with a fold down the length of the cloth. Cut your white tree fabric into 1 strip 1½″ × 15½″, 1 strip 1½″ × 6½″, 1 strip 1½″ × 10½″, and 1 strip 1½″ × 13½″. Press under a ¼″ seam allowance on the two long sides of each of these strips. Pin the longest strip over the center crease of the background fabric and 5″ down from your top raw edge. Lay the 1½″ × 6½″ strip across this band horizontally 1½″ from the top edge of this strip. Pin in place and blindstitch the long sides of these strips to the back-

ground. The raw edges of the bands will be covered with an appliqué.

The second horizontal band, 1½″ × 10½″, will be positioned and sewn 4″ down from the previous horizontal band. The last strip, 1½″ × 13½″, will be spaced 4″ from the middle strip. Blindstitch or topstitch the bands to the background by machine.

■ **2.** Transfer your appliqué designs to template material. Blindstitch 2 eggs to the top branch, 4 to the second, and 6 to the lowest branch. Position hearts over the ends of your branches and the bunny on the treetop. Machinesew together 4 strips of varied prints 1½″ × 6″ and press. Cut the flowerpot from this cloth, and blindstitch in place.

■ **3.** This quilt is framed by a 1½″ strip of print that matches the striped border fabric in color. This print is also used for the binding. Cut 4 strips of the framing fabric 1½″ × 23½″, and 2 strips 1½″ × 19½″. Sew strips to the long sides of your quilt and press. Complete the border by stitching the remaining strips to the top and lower edges. Press.

■ **4.** Cut 4 border bands from your strips. The border in this quilt was cut 3½″ wide. When using a stripe it is important to accommodate the width of the striped design. Cut the stripe width to complete the design, and remember to add ¼″ seam allow-

ance beyond the printed repeat. Two of the border sections are 24½″ long and 2 are 32″ long. These are cut for the finished length of the quilt, which will allow for a mitered corner treatment. Sew your borders to the edge of the quilt. Press.

■ **5.** Layer the top, batting, and backing for quilting. Baste the layers for machine or hand quilting. Quilt around the appliqués, and mark and quilt the background in a diagonal grid of 1½″. Quilt the border following the design elements of your stripe. With the batting in place, you will find it easier to add your embroidery. Pull the threads through to the batting layer only, and secure them with a small backstitch. The bunny requires a small nose and eye. Apply a touch of blush on his cheeks and ears with a cotton swab. The eggs are secured with a single layer of ribbon floss. Lace is added to the top band of the flowerpot.

■ **6.** When the quilting is complete, bind the edges with the strips cut 1½″ in width. If this is used as a wallhanging, bind the edges with strips cut lengthwise along the grain to ensure a straight edge. For use as a small carriage or crib covering, bind the edges with bias-cut strips for greatest durability.

Patterns for this design are on the next page.

Egg Tree

(continued)

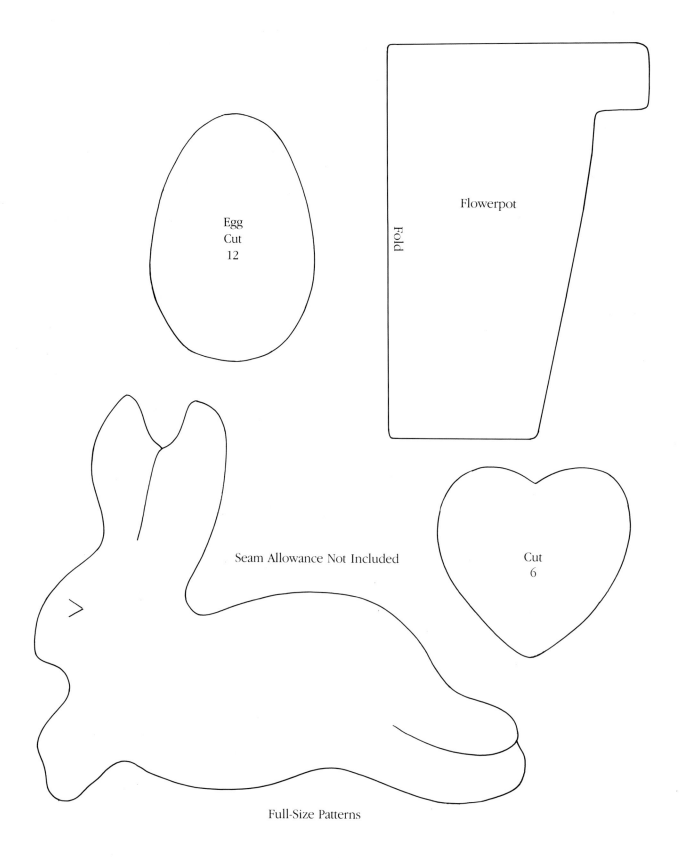

Egg
Cut
12

Flowerpot

Fold

Cut
6

Seam Allowance Not Included

Full-Size Patterns

f o u r

country hearts

Time Frame 2

Finished size: 32″ × 43½″

Materials required

¼ yard turquoise solid
¼ yard white-on-white print
1 yard pink print for border and
  binding
1 yard turquoise print for border
Assorted scraps for heart sections
1¼ yards backing
Baby-sized batting
Matching sewing and quilting threads

■ **1.** Enlarge and transfer the patterns for your hearts to template material. Each heart will be made from 3 sections. Mark on the right side of the fabric and add ¼″ seam allowance as you cut them with your scissors. Start by stitching the top left and right sides together on their seamline, and complete the heart by machine- or hand-stitching the lower unit. Press. Once your heart is completed, baste under the seam allowance and press. This quilt will require 12 hearts. When working with scraps you must take care to achieve a balance in color and texture. Select each fabric comparing it to others as you work along. The hearts are appliquéd to the white background fabric, which is cut into twelve 6″ squares. Note that half the hearts point to the lower

right corner of the squares and half point to the lower left corner of the squares. After blindstitching, trim away the excess background fabric beneath each heart, leaving a ¼″ seam allowance of the background fabric.

■ **2.** This quilt is assembled in a block arrangement. Cut twelve 6″ squares from your turquoise solid fabric. Alternate 2 heart squares with 2 turquoise solid for the block construction. Refer to the photograph. When 6 blocks are completed you are ready to assemble the quilt. Cut your pink print into 7 strips 1½″ × 36″. Sew a pink strip between 2 blocks and to the outside edge of each row. Trim the pink strip even to the block edges. Stitch pink to the top edge and between the rows to assemble the quilt. Stitch pink to the lower edge and press.

■ **3.** The outside border is cut into 2 bands 3½″ × 26½″ and 2 bands 3½″ × 43½″. Cut these lengthwise along the grain of your fabric. Sew the top and lower bands on first, and the long sides to complete the assembly. Press.

■ **4.** Layer the top, batting, and backing. Baste the layers for machine or hand quilting. Quilt around the appliqués. Quilt 4

small hearts in the center of the solid squares. Use the heart template provided in the Egg Tree quilt, page 50. Scatter the quilted heart motif around the border for a simple quilting design.

■ **5.** When the quilting is complete, bind the quilt with the pink print.

Finished quilt is shown on the next page.

Half-Size Pattern

Seam Allowance Not Included

the little sleepy railroad

Time Frame 2

. . .

Finished size: 29½″ × 37½″

Materials required

⅔ yard gray print for background
⅝ yard print for second border
*½ yard green print for first border and
    binding*
*Assorted scraps for appliqués in black
    and primary colors*
1 yard tear-away stabilizer
1 yard backing
Baby-sized batting
Matching sewing and quilting threads
*Optional: Six 1½″ buttons for train
    wheels and small bell for engine*

■ **1.** Cut background print 27½″ × 19½″.

■ **2.** Enlarge and transfer patterns for engine and smoke to template material. The two cars are cut from rectangles of fabric 4″ × 3½″; this does not include seam allowance. Machine- or hand-appliqué the cars to your background, positioning the train 6¼″ from the lower edge.

■ **3.** Machine-appliqué with a tear-away stabilizer. The two front wheels of the engine are circles 1½″ in diameter; the back wheel is 2″ in diameter. Once your stitching is completed, tear off the stabilizer. For hand embroidery, mark the circles and backstitch with 2 strands of floss on the marked lines.

■ **4.** Cut 3 crossgrain strips for first border fabric, 1½″ × 44″. Sew a strip to each of the short sides of your quilt, and complete attachment by sewing the bands to the

top and lower edges. The final border is cut 4½″ in width. To minimize stretch to the outer edge, the border should all be cut lengthwise along the grain. Note in the photograph that the fabric used on the border, the train motif, had a design that ran lengthwise on the fabric. Cutting all the borders lengthwise would have positioned the trains in the border on their side. I therefore cut 2 borders crossgrain. The edge was stabilized by cutting the binding 1½″ in width from the lengthwise grain of the fabric.

■ **5.** Layer the top, batting, and backing for quilting. Baste the lay-

ers for machine or hand quilting. I machine-quilted this quilt following line elements that enhanced the picture. I quilted smoke coming from the train and tracks under the train. Over the top of the picture, I wrote in quilting, "Choo, Choo, Choo!" The lesson in quilting is to experiment and do your own thing! When all the quilting is completed, bind the quilt.

■ **6.** After the quilt is finished, securely attach the buttons and a small bell for the engine.

Finished quilt is shown on the next page.

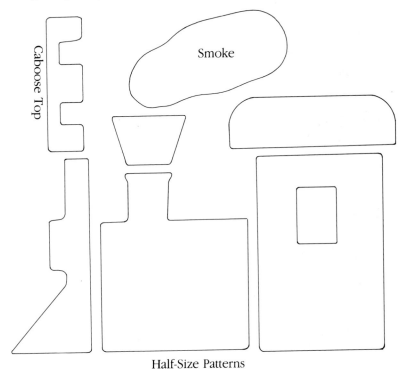

Half-Size Patterns

Seam Allowance Not Included

The Little Sleepy Railroad
(continued)

little bear's sunny day

Time Frame 2

Finished size: 31½″ × 41½″

Materials required

25½″ × 35½″ print for background
1 yard print for border
¼ yard brown print for bear
3 primary-color solids or prints for
balloon appliqués
10″ × 8″ scrap of white piqué for
cloud
⅛ yard green print for corner squares
Assorted scraps of red prints for corner
hearts
Assorted yellow scraps for sun appliqués
Ribbon floss
1¼ yards backing
½ yard red print for binding
Baby-sized batting
Matching sewing and quilting threads

■ **1.** Enlarge and transfer patterns to template material. Mark the appliqués on the right side of your fabrics, and add ¼″ seam allowance when cutting. Baste under the seam allowance on the appliqué edges that will not be overlayed by another appliqué. The bear's neck will be overlayed by the head, so it is unnecessary to baste this raw edge under.

■ **2.** Position the bear approximately 6″ from the lower right-hand corner of the background and 6″ from the right side. Pin the body in place, placing the head and left arm over the body. The right ear should be positioned under the head. Blindstitch these sec-

tions. Cut 2 layers of the left ear, adding ¼″ seam allowance. Stitch the 2 layers together along their curved line, leaving the lower straight side open. Reverse the ear. Turning under the lower edge, appliqué the lower ear edge to the bear. This creates a three-dimensional effect.

■ **3.** Mark and baste the balloon appliqués. Center these on the background, referring to the photograph as a guide. Mark and baste the cloud and sun appliqués. Note that the lower edges of all the sun sections will be overlayed by the cloud, so do not baste their seam allowance under. Position the cloud with the lower edge about 10″ from the top background and 3″ from the right side. Blindstitch these appliqués in place.

■ **4.** Cut borders: 2 strips 3½″ × 35½″ and 2 strips 3½″ × 25½″. Cut these lengthwise along the grain to eliminate stretch. Cut 4 accent corner squares 3½″. Sew the long strips to the quilt sides. Attach a square to either side of the short strips, and complete the border attachment by seaming these units across the top and lower quilt edges. Press.

■ **5.** Transfer the heart pattern to an assortment of pink and red fabrics. Prepare 20 hearts, marked and basted. Freezer paper appliqué is an excellent method for

this shape. Refer to the Glossary for more detailed instruction. Scatter 5 hearts in each corner, overlapping the border seams and curving into the quilt background. Blindstitch and press. Cut the background layer out from under your appliqués, leaving ¼″ seam allowance. Press.

■ **6.** Layer the quilt, batting, and backing. Baste the quilt for hand or machine appliqué. I quilted by following the outline of each appliqué and filling the background with vertical stitching 2″ apart. I used the heart motif scattered randomly in the border as a quilting design.

■ **7.** When quilting is complete, bind the raw edges with strips cut 1½″ in width.

■ **8.** Embellish this quilt by attaching ribbon floss from the balloons to the bear's paw. A tied bow of the 3 floss streamers is an attractive touch. Embroider the nose and eye with black floss, using 1 or 2 strands. The cheek was colored with fabric crayon. These small touches will bring your little bear to life!

Finished quilt and patterns for this design
are on the next two pages.

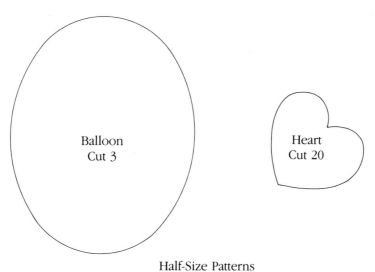

Balloon
Cut 3

Heart
Cut 20

Half-Size Patterns

Seam Allowance Not Included

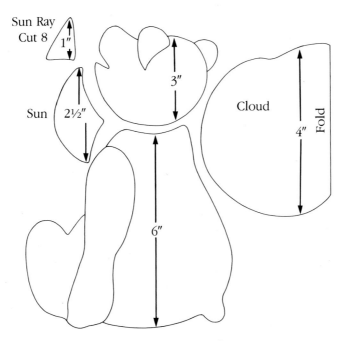

Sun Ray
Cut 8

1"

Sun

2½"

3"

6"

Cloud

Fold

4"

Enlarge Patterns to Sizes Indicated

Seam Allowance Not Included

sweet baby quilt

Time Frame 3

Finished size: 36″ × 40″

Materials required

24½″ × 28½″ print for background
1½ yards yellow floral print for third
  border
¼ yard yellow print strip for first
  border
1 yard orange print for second border
  and binding
Four 5″ × 7″ calico prints for letters
Assorted calico print scraps for duck,
  bunny, rattle, and bow appliqués
1 yard backing
Baby-sized batting
Matching sewing and quilting threads

■ **1.** Enlarge and transfer appliqués to template material. The appliqués for this design are well suited to a freezer paper appliqué method.

■ **2.** Prepare the appliqués for hand appliqué. Position the appliqués in a pleasing manner, referring to the photograph. Blindstitch the appliqués to the background.

■ **3.** Cut yellow print strips for the first border of the quilt, two 1½″ × 24½″ and two 1½″ × 30½″. Sew the strips to the sides of the quilt first, then attach the top and lower border bands. The orange second border will require 2 strips cut 2″ × 30½″ and 2 strips 2″ × 26½″. Sew these to the quilt following the same order as the first border. The top piecing is completed by stitching the last border, 4″ × 33½″, and 4″ × 36½″. The yellow floral border should be cut lengthwise along the grain of

your fabric to minimize stretching. Press.

■ **4.** Layer the quilt, batting, and backing. Baste the quilt for hand or machine quilting. Quilt around the individual appliqués. I drew a 2″ diamond grid in the border sections for quilting this area. These quilting motifs were quick to complete and are appropriate for hand or machine quilting.

■ **5.** When your quilting is completed, finish the raw edges with binding cut 1½″ from the orange print.

Half-Size Patterns

Seam Allowance Not Included

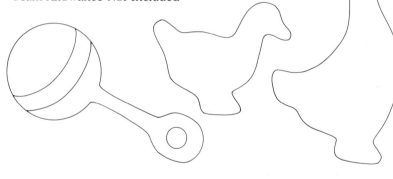

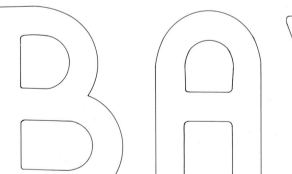

Enlarge All Letters to 6″ High

59

e i g h t

sea life

Time Frame 3

· · ·

Finished size: 33½" × 41½"

Materials required

1 yard print for border

5 assorted background prints or solids that will coordinate with the border print: eight 8½" squares and two 8½" × 16½" rectangles. Repeating the background prints will provide a uniformity to the design.

Assorted scraps for appliqué patterns in black, teal, orange, yellow, pink, and peach. Repeating these fabrics in different shapes will also tie the design together.

Fusible adhesive for machine appliqué

1 yard tear-away stabilizer

1¼ yards backing

½ yard print for binding

Baby-sized batting

Matching quilting and sewing threads

■ **1.** Cut 8 background squares 8½" in size. Cut 2 background rectangles 8½" × 16½". Assemble the quilt background, starting with the left vertical row, sewing a rectangle above 2 squares. The middle row is a reversal of the left vertical row, with 2 squares on the top and 1 rectangle below them. The right vertical row is constructed of four 8½" squares sewn together. Assemble the rows referring to photograph. Press.

■ **2.** Enlarge and transfer the appliqué patterns to a fusible adhesive following the manufacturer's directions for machine appliqué. For hand appliqué, use a freezer paper method as detailed in the Glossary. For machine appliqué, stabilize the background with a tear-away stabilizer as you satin-stitch. Use accent threads to add detail to the appliqués. When executing this design by hand, embroider the details after the quilt

is layered. This enables you to catch thread ends in the batting.

■ **3.** Cut 4 border strips lengthwise along the grain, 32½" × 4½". Sew the side borders on first, and complete the assembly by sewing the top and lower borders in place. Press.

■ **4.** Layer the quilt top, batting, and backing. Baste the quilt for hand or machine quilting. Quilt around the appliqués, and follow the seams of the background. On the solid background blocks I quilted a 1½" grid design for variety. If your background prints have an interesting pattern, follow it as a convenient quilting motif.

■ **5.** When all the quilting is completed, bind the edges with binding strips cut 1½" wide.

Patterns for this design are on the next page.

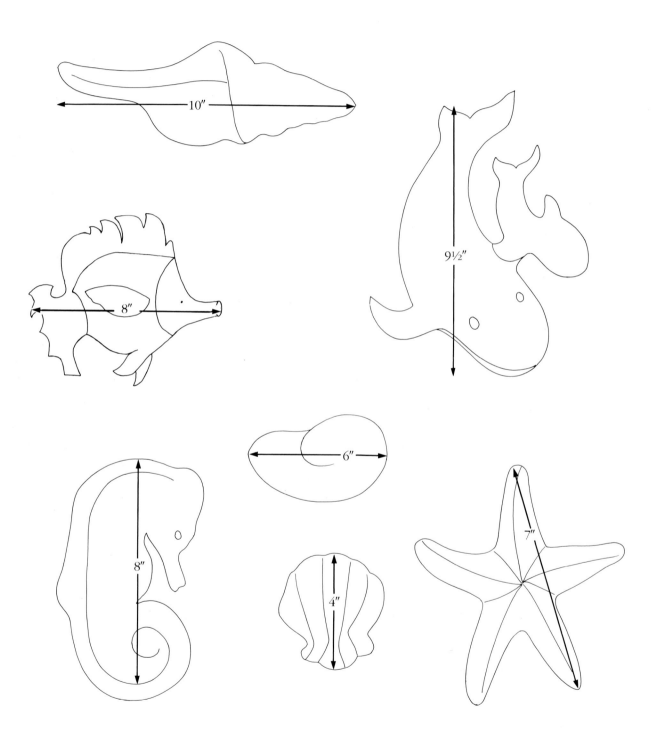

10"

8"

9½"

8"

6"

4"

7"

Seam Allowance Not Included

Enlarge Patterns to Sizes Indicated

mouse to tower

Time Frame 3

Finished size: 34″ × 40″

Materials required

18½″ × 18½″ blue solid fabric for
*   background*
1 yard print for border
84 assorted 3½″ squares for border.
*   Select an assortment of shades of*
*   red, white, and blue that vary in*
*   value.*
¼ yard red print for airplane appliqué
⅛ yard white for cloud appliqués
3 scraps of light, medium, and dark
*   brown prints for mouse head, face,*
*   paws, and jacket*
Scraps of red solid fabric for propeller
*   and plane interior*
1 yard backing
Baby-sized batting
½ yard red print for binding
Matching sewing and quilting threads
Black cotton embroidery floss
Red fabric crayon

■ **1.** Using template material, transfer the 3½″ template square from the Eyelet and Lace quilt, page 15. (This measurement includes ¼″ seam allowance.) You will need 84 of these squares for the outer patchwork border. Select a wide assortment of light, medium, and dark prints from red, white, and blue fabric. A variety of values will make the border interesting. Sew 2 rows of 6 squares together. Sew these vertically to ei-

ther side of the center 18½″ background square. The top and lower rows are made of 10 squares across. Three rows of these 10 units are seamed together and attached across the top and lower edges. Refer to photograph for placement. Press.

■ **2.** Enlarge the appliqués to the size indicated using a copy machine. Using masking tape, secure the picture to a flat surface, and lay your quilt top over the design. The design lines should show through your fabric surface. Use a light source to shine through the back of your fabric if you have difficulty seeing through it. Transfer the outer marking lines using a marker or pencil. This will serve as a guide for positioning your appliqués.

■ **3.** Transfer your individual appliqués to tracing paper. Prepare your appliqués using your favorite method as discussed in the Glossary. Lay the appliqués on the background in an appropriate layered order. For example, the lower cloud and the airplane fuselage should be positioned at the same time. The lower wing should be placed over the fuselage, overlapping the cloud. Blindstitch the appliqués to the background.

Maintaining ¼″ seam allowance, remove background fabric from under your appliqués. Embroider features on the mouse using 1 strand of black embroidery floss with a simple backstitch. The eyes and nose are satin-stitched. Additional life is added to the mouse face with a light brushing of red fabric crayon or blush. Practice on a sample cloth to achieve the shade you prefer.

■ **4.** Cut outside borders: two 2½″ × 36½″ and two 2½″ × 34½″. Sew the bands to the long sides. Press. Complete the assembly by seaming the bands to the top and lower edges. Press.

■ **5.** Layer the quilt top, batting, and backing. Baste the quilt for hand or machine quilting. Quilt around the appliqués and following the patchwork border. I filled in the background of my center panel with quilted clouds and air currents. Experiment with your quilting and stitch these sections as you please.

■ **6.** When the top is completely quilted, bind the edges with red print binding cut 1½″ wide.

Finished quilt and patterns for this design
are shown on the next two pages.

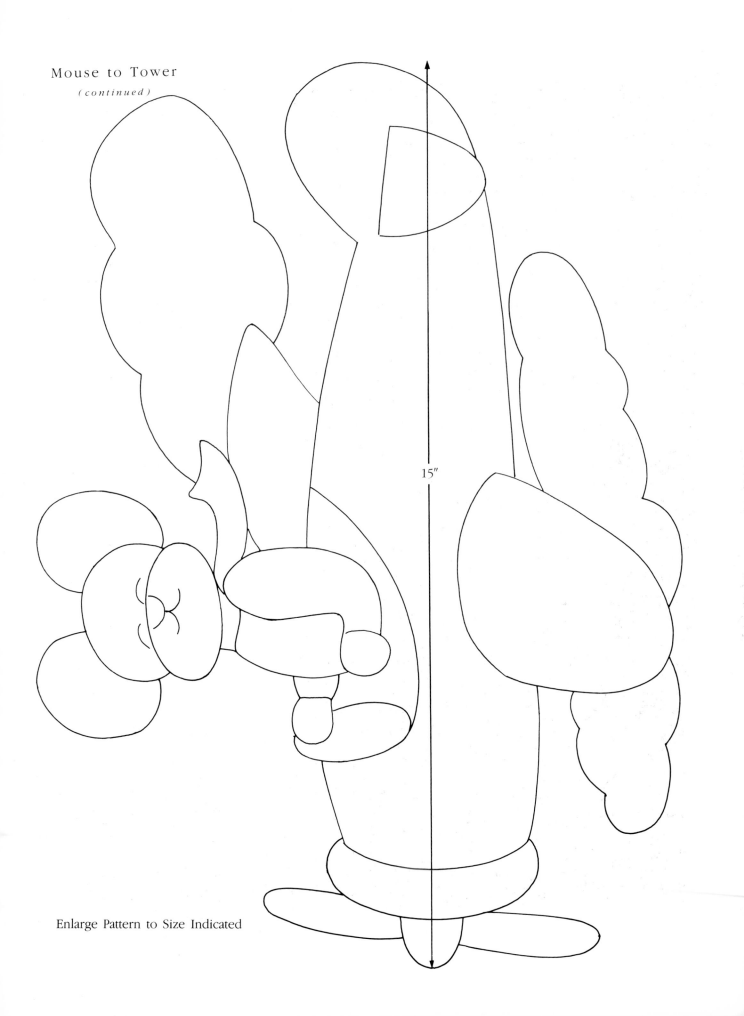

Mouse to Tower
(continued)

15″

Enlarge Pattern to Size Indicated

t e n

carousel

Time Frame 3

. . .

Finished size: 40″ × 48½″

Materials required

1¼ yards background fabric
1 yard red print for border
1 yard blue print for border
½ yard white print for horse
½ yard fusible medium-weight
*   interfacing*
¼ yard of four solids or prints for
*   awning border*
Scraps of less than ⅛ yard for bridle,
*   saddle, saddlecloth, mane, tail,*
*   hooves, and heart appliqués*
⅛ yard silver or gold fabric for pole
Decorative large-motif flowers cut from
*   chintz or large-print calico*
Fusible adhesive
Tear-away stabilizer
1 yard backing
Baby-sized batting
Matching sewing and quilting threads

■ **1.** Enlarge patterns to sizes indicated using a copy machine. Transfer the patterns to tracing paper. This design can be appliquéd by hand or machine. For handwork, add a scant ¼″ seam allowance and proceed according to the additional instructions in the Glossary. The directions that follow are given for machine appliqué, as the original quilt was completed in this manner. Use a fusible adhesive as a convenient method of placing the many appliqués on the background. To trace the design on the parchment covering of the fusible adhesive, reverse the tracing of your pattern. Trace the horse, saddle, saddlecloth, mane, hooves, and tail on the parchment

through the transparent adhesive. Add the appliqué numbers as well to each section for ease in identification.

■ **2.** In order to prevent the background from showing through the white fabric for your horse, you may find it necessary to fuse a layer of interfacing to the wrong side of the white fabric. Follow the manufacturer's directions to do this.

■ **3.** Cut your background fabric 32½″ × 41½″. Press a crease down the length of your background 12″ from the left side. This will be the position for the pole, which will be cut 1¼″ × 32″. You may attach the pole with glue, fusible webbing, or straight stitching to the background before passing over the raw edges with a satin stitch. Position the left edge of the pole on the crease line and secure the pole in place. Before stitching, place a tear-away stabilizer under the wrong side of your fabric. This will eliminate puckering as you stitch. Refer to your sewing machine manual for the proper settings for a satin stitch. Use a matching thread, and satin-stitch only the long sides of the pole.

■ **4.** You are now ready to position the horse. Iron the traced horse attached to your fusible adhesive to the wrong side of your white fabric. Cut it on the lines and peel the parchment off as the manufacturer recommends. Position the horse tilted upright with the

head at the highest point. Refer to the photograph as a guide. The pole should enter at the middle of the saddle and reappear between the rear legs. Press and fuse to your background. In a similar manner, cut and fuse the mane, tail, saddle, saddlecloth, and hooves. The bridle should be traced from the head in one piece and fused. Select large flowers from the chintz or calico fabric and fuse these to embellish your horse. Satin-stitch with a tear-away stabilizer beneath all your layers.

■ **5.** Cut 2 bands of both of your border fabrics 2½″ × 41½″. Cut 2 bands of both your border fabrics 2½″ × 40½″. Sew the 2 border bands together as one unit, and attach this to one long side of the quilt. Repeat this for the second long side. Press. Join 2 bands together for the lower edge, and seam this in place.

■ **6.** Cut the awning sections for the quilt using the patterns provided. Sew the 6 sections together by machine, matching notches. Baste the lower curved edge under ⅛″. Position the straight top edge of the awning even with top edge of the quilt. Blindstitch the sides and lower curved edge to the quilt top by hand or machine. Sew the assembled top border bands to the top edge. Your seam will be joining the border, awning top, and background in one seam. Press. Cut out excess background fabric under the appliquéd awning layer. Maintain ¼" seam allowance of the background fabric under the appliqué.

■ **7.** Appliqué the hearts to the top of the awning. Press.

■ **8.** Position the top, batting, and background together. Pin and baste the 3 layers for hand or machine quilting. Quilt around the appliqués. I machine-quilted around the clouds in my back ground fabric. When using a solid background, quilt a diamond grid pattern as a filler. Draw lines parallel to the angular awning, and quilt these at 1" intervals. Quilt "in the ditch" along the seamlines of the borders to complete.

■ **9.** When the quilting is completed, finish the outer edges by binding with a contrasting 1½"-wide band of strips cut on the bias or lengthwise. Sew a 3" sleeve to the top backing. Insert a café curtain rod or a stained dowel for an easy quilt hanger.

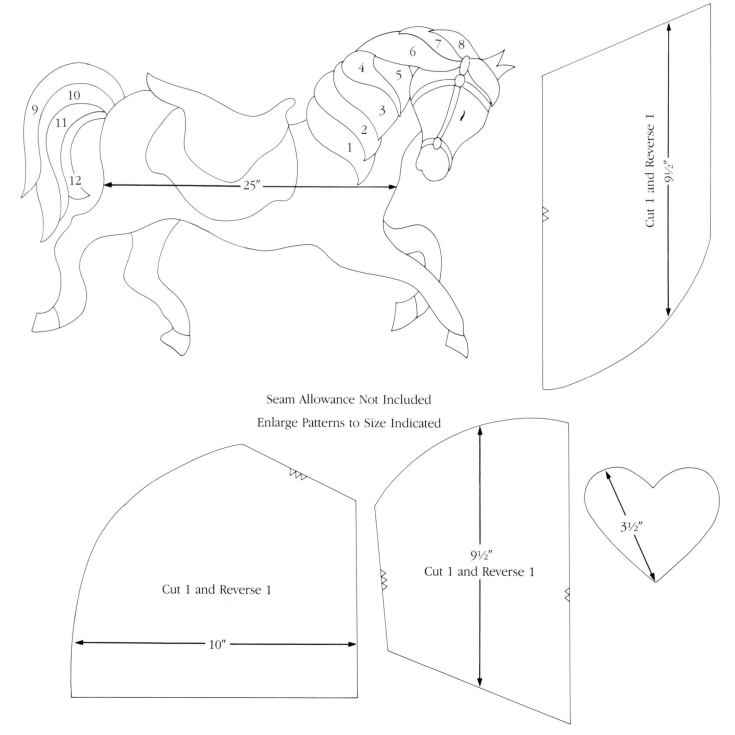

Seam Allowance Not Included

Enlarge Patterns to Size Indicated

t h r e e

Mixed Blessings

Beginner quilters often have preferences in technique. Some enjoy piecing on the machine, and select patchwork designs exclusively. Hand stitchers want portable projects to stitch while sharing an evening with their family. Appliqué answers their needs. With exploration in quilting, these two camps merge, discovering the appeal of both methods. Some projects demand completion in one or two days; strip piecing is the answer. There will be times when you seek the ongoing pleasure of a challenging project. A special addition to the family may demand a unique quilt to mark the occasion. Whatever the circumstance, combining appliqué with patchwork is the theme of this last set of designs. Many of the quilts combine new ingredients with patterns previously presented. As you gain command of the skills and patterns, you will be ready to create your own sampler, as illustrated by the final quilt, Mixed Blessings. With the basic principles of construction and pattern variety, designing is not beyond your skill level. I hope these projects will open the door to designing many quilts in the future.

little bear's first star

Time Frame 1

Finished size: 24″ × 24″

Materials required

½ yard blue print for border
⅛ yard red print for corner squares
⅛ yard blue print for corners
¼ yard light brown calico for bear
  appliqué
About ⅛ yard each of 5 calico prints
  ranging from dark to light for
  background patchwork
6″ scrap of yellow for star appliqué
¾ yard calico backing
½ yard blue print for binding
¾ yard batting
Matching sewing and quilting threads
Brown embroidery floss

▪ **1.** Enlarge and trace the 3½″ square pattern from the Eyelet and Lace quilt, page 15. (This measurement includes ¼″ seam allowance.) Transfer this to your template material. The 5 calico prints you have selected for the background should range in value from light to dark. None of these prints should be used as your border fabric. Assign numbers to these fabrics: 1 being the darkest, 2 the second darkest, and so forth, with 5 the lightest of the values. Label the fabrics for ease in identification. Cut 8 squares from fabric 1, 10 from fabric 2, 8 from fabric 3, 6 from fabric 4, and 4 from fabric 5.

▪ **2.** With the piecing diagram as a guide, assemble the rows horizontally, and finally seam the rows together. Press.

▪ **3.** Cut 4 border strips 3½″ ×

18½″ lengthwise along the grain of your fabric. Sew 2 borders to opposite sides of the quilt. The corner-accent nine patches should be cut from a red print and from a different blue print than the border fabric. Cut three 1½″ × 12″ strips of each of the fabrics used in this square. Sew 3 strips together down the 12″ side, with 2 blues on the outside and red in the center. Reverse this order, with the reds on the outside and blue in the center, for a second grouping. Press and cut these strips into 1½″ bands. To assemble the nine-patch square, refer to nine-patch diagram for clarification. Press the 4 squares once assembled. Sew a square to the top and lower edges of the remaining side borders. Seam the final border units to the quilt to complete the background assembly.

▪ **4.** The bear pattern for this quilt is found in the Little Bear's Sunny Day quilt, page 57. Transfer the bear pattern to your brown print using freezer paper appliqué or traditional appliqué; both methods are discussed in the Glossary. Position your bear sections with the lower body sections slightly into the border. Pin or baste in place, and blindstitch the bear to the background. Position the right ear under the head. The neck overlaps the top of the body. Blindstitch these sections. Trace 2 of the left ear pattern on the wrong side of the bear fabric. Use 2 lay-

ers of your fabric and sew right sides together, stitching on the curved ear line only. Cut the ear out of the 2 layers, adding ⅛″ seam allowance to the curved side and a full ¼″ seam allowance to the lower opening edge. Reverse and close the ear, turning the seam allowance inside. Press. Appliqué the lower ear edge to the bear's head. This will give the ear a three-dimensional effect, flipping away from the bear's body.

▪ **5.** Transfer the star pattern to the yellow fabric. Cut a scant ¼″ seam allowance, and turn the seam under with your needle as you blindstitch the star to the background. It will be necessary to clip into the inside angles of the star to maintain the shape.

▪ **6.** Layer the quilt top with the batting and backing. Baste the layers for machine or hand quilting. Quilt around the appliqués. Quilt the background by following the outline of the squares. I used metallic thread and machine-quilted straight stitches from the star to the bear in a random arrangement to emphasize a starlight effect.

▪ **7.** When all the quilting is completed, finish the raw edges with blue print binding. A 3″ sleeve can be sewn to the top backing for hanging this quilt on a wall. Insert a stained dowel or a curtain rod to hang.

Patterns for this design are on the next page.

Little Bear's First Star
(continued)

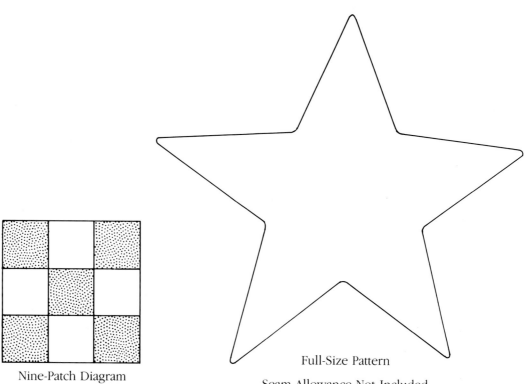

Nine-Patch Diagram

Full-Size Pattern

Seam Allowance Not Included

1	2	3	4	5	1
2	1	2	3	4	5
3	2	1	2	3	4
4	3	2	1	2	3
5	4	3	2	1	2
1	5	4	3	2	1

Piecing Diagram

rainbow daisy

Time Frame 2

Finished size: 34″ × 44½″

Materials required

1 yard royal blue print for squares and border
1 yard light print for squares and border
¼ yard each of 4 assorted yellow prints (45″-wide fabric)
¼ yard each of 4 assorted red prints (45″-wide fabric)
¼ yard each of 4 assorted green prints (45″-wide fabric)
¼ yard each of 4 assorted orange prints (45″-wide fabric)
1 yard backing
½ yard red print for binding
Baby-sized batting
Matching sewing and quilting threads

■ **1.** Cut out six 6½″ squares from the light background print. This includes the ¼″ seam allowance. Mark the appliqué petals on the right side of your prints and cut them adding a scant ¼″ seam allowance. Each daisy will require 6 assorted colored petals. Crease the background square into quarters to determine the centerpoint. Position the appliqués around this point and blindstitch them with matching thread.

■ **2.** Cut 24 triangles from your blue print using template A . Sew these to each side of the squares. Press.

■ **3.** Cut 1 strip from each of your yellow prints 1⅝″ × 45″. Seam these strips together along their 45″ length using ¼″ seam allowance. Press flat. Using template B, cut 7 triangles from the pieced yellow band, keeping the diagonal of the triangles along the outside edge. Repeat this process for the red, green, and orange prints. Sew the B triangles to the outside edge of the block unit. Seam the B triangles as the photograph indicates, with red in the top right corner, orange in the lower right corner, green in the lower left corner, and yellow at the top left corner. Each square is assembled in the same manner. Press.

■ **4.** Seam your blocks together in rows of 2. Sew the 3 horizontal rows together to complete the center of the quilt.

■ **5.** You will have 1 triangle of each color group remaining for the border treatment. Sew the red and yellow together along their short side. Sew the orange and green together in the same manner. Baste or press under the outside ¼″ seam allowance on the long diagonal of each triangle. Position the pair at the center seamline of the top and lower edges of your quilt. Sew the pairs to this edge. Before proceeding to the first light border, fold the accent-triangle pair into the body of the quilt and safety-pin them onto the body of the quilt. This will keep them out of your way as you work.

■ **6.** Cut the light border lengthwise along the grain of your fabric. Cut 2 strips 3½″ × 36½″ and 2 strips 3½″ × 30½″. Sew the border to the sides of the quilt first. Complete the first border attachment by seaming the strips to the top and lower edges. This final attachment should sew through the accent triangles as well as your quilt edge.

■ **7.** Cut the second border lengthwise along the grain also. Cut 2 strips 2½″ × 42½″ and 2 strips 2½″ × 36½″. Sew the side borders on first, and complete the assembly by sewing the borders to the top and lower edges.

■ **8.** Unpin the accent triangles and blindstitch the outside diagonal edges to the border bands. Cut away the background border fabrics from under the accent triangles, leaving ¼″ seam allowance of the background fabrics within the appliquéd triangles. Press.

■ **9.** Layer the quilt top, batting, and backing. Pin the layers for hand or machine quilting. Quilt around the appliqués and down the centerline of each strip.

■ **10.** When all the quilting is completed, bind the raw edges with red print.

Finished quilt and patterns for this design are on the next two pages.

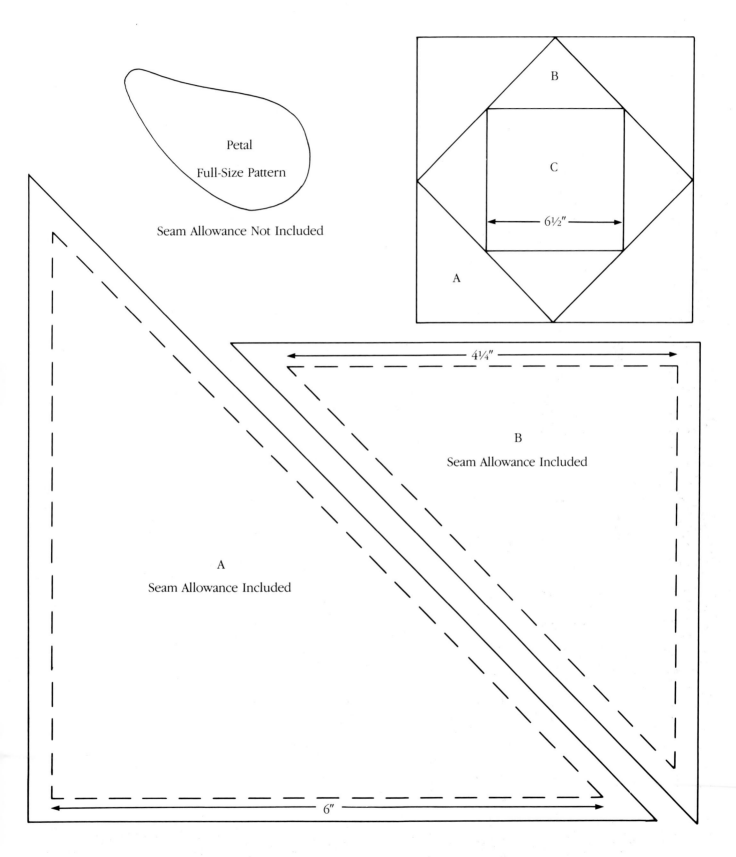

Petal
Full-Size Pattern

Seam Allowance Not Included

B

C

6½″

A

4¼″

B
Seam Allowance Included

A
Seam Allowance Included

6″

t h r e e

honey bear

Time Frame 2

• • •

Finished size: 27″ × 27″

Materials required

¾ yard lavender print for border and blocks
1 yard light print for blocks and binding
¼ yard each of 5 assorted solids
¼ yard light tan for bear
⅛ yard medium tan for bear pads, paws, and ears
Scraps of rose, yellow print, and gold
⅛ yard light print for bear muzzle and honey jar label
¾ yard backing
¾ yard batting
Matching sewing and quilting threads
Black and brown embroidery floss
2 pom-poms

■ **1.** The background of the quilt combines 4 blocks of the traditional Honey Bee quilt pattern. This pattern is a variation of an extended nine patch. Start by cutting 3 strips 2½″ × 22″ from each of the 2 prints used in the background. Sew these strips into 2 arrangements using ¼″ seam allowance. The first band should place the light print on either side of the lavender print. The second arrangement should reverse this order, with the 2 lavender print strips to either side of a light strip. Press the strips with the seam folded to the lavender print. Cut the bands into segments of 2½″. Referring to the block diagram, select 2 segments with the medium on the outside of the band for the top and lower rows of the nine patch. A middle row of a light/medium/light segment completes the block. Make 4 blocks for the quilt. Press.

■ **2.** Cut 2 strips 2½″ × 44″ crossgrain from the light background fabric. Sew a light strip to one side of each of the 4 blocks. Cut this band even with the block raw edge. Repeat this procedure, attaching a band to the opposite side of the blocks. From each of the 5 solid fabrics cut four 2½″ squares. Cut the light background into eight 2½″ × 6½″ sections. Sew 1 of the solid squares to either side of two 6½″ × 2½″ bands. Seam this to the top and lower edges of the block. Repeat this procedure, sewing 3 different colored solid squares to the remaining 3 blocks. Use the block diagram as a guide.

■ **3.** Sew the 4 blocks together, 2 across and 2 rows down. Press.

■ **4.** Cut 4 border bands from the lavender fabric 3½″ × 20½″. I used a one-way printed fabric for this quilt. To maintain the pattern, which is similar to a stripe, it was necessary to cut 2 of the borders, for the sides, lengthwise along the grain and 2, for the top and lower edges, crossgrain.

■ **5.** The corner squares are constructed in the same manner as the quilt blocks. The completed nine-patch corner blocks are 3″ squares. Cut three 1½″ strips from one of the solid fabrics used in this small block and three 1½″ lavender strips. (These measurements include ¼″ seam allowance.) The bands can be cut about 9″ in length, providing just a sufficient quantity for each lavender corner combination. Sew 3 bands together, 1 with the lavender print on the outside and a solid in the middle, and 1 with the second solid on the outside and the lavender print in the middle. Press and cut these into 1½″ segments. Seam these into your nine-patch corner blocks. Refer to photograph for finished effect. Repeat this procedure for each of the 4 corner units. Sew the nine-patch squares to either side of the top and lower border bands, then to the two sides of the quilt top.

■ **6.** Transfer the teardrop shape to template material for appliquéing. Blindstitch 3 teardrops in each of the 4 corners of the quilt.

■ **7.** Enlarge and transfer the bear pattern to the fabric. The bear is one large shape, with the muzzle, bow, paws, and feet sewn to the body. The honey pot is also blindstitched to the lower bear body. Transfer the small appliqué sections to the fabric and blindstitch in place.

■ **8.** Trace around the bear's left ear on the wrong side of the medium-tan bear fabric. Position a second layer with right sides together under this marked piece, and sew on the curved line. Leave the lower edge open for reversing. Trim ¼″ off the seam allowance and reverse through the lower edge. Position this ear section at the bear head, overlapping the head over the ear raw edge. Blindstitch the bear in place, leaving the top of the ear free for a three-dimensional effect.

■ **9.** Embroider the details on the bear. The eyes and nose are satin-stitched with 2 strands of floss. The body is stitched down the chest and side of the head with a small running stitch. The mouth is made with 1 thread of black and a back-stitch. Keep the stitch length short to maintain the curved lines. The jar label is stitched with straight stitches.

■ **10.** Layer the top, batting, and backing together. Baste the layers for hand or machine quilting. Quilt around the appliqués, and use a traditional wreath quilting pattern over the blocks as a motif.

■ **11.** When all the quilting is completed, bind the edges with the light print to finish.

■ **12.** The little bee that is attached to the honey pot was made by seaming 2 pom-poms together for the body. The wings were traced on fusible adhesive and attached to 2 layers of white fabric. Before cutting the shapes out, embroider a satin stitch on the wing edges. Trim to the satin-stitching line when the embroidery is completed. Use a soluble stabilizer under your embroidery. Once you have completed the stitches, cut the wings out. Wet the wings to dissolve the stabilizer, which washes away leaving a starched finish to the embroidery. Sew the wings to the pom-pom body, and attach the completed bee to the quilt. This is appropriate for a wall quilt treatment, and not suitable for crib use.

Enlarge Pattern to Size Indicated

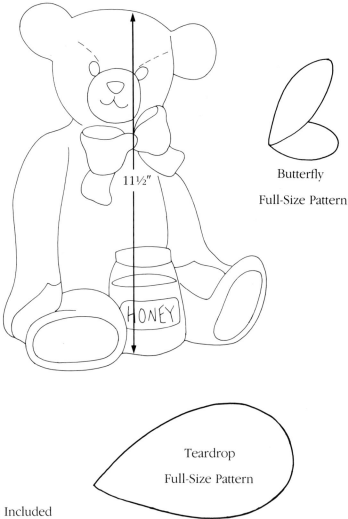

11½"

Butterfly

Full-Size Pattern

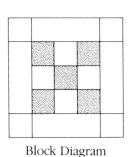

Block Diagram

Teardrop

Full-Size Pattern

Seam Allowance Not Included

nine-patch kitties

Time Frame 2

●　●　●

Finished size: 33″ × 41″

Materials required

1 yard light print for border and
square
½ yard green solid for binding and
first border
⅛ yard each of 8 varied calico prints
for the nine-patch blocks
6 assorted scraps of yellow prints for
cat appliqués
1¼ yards backing
Baby-sized batting
Matching sewing and quilting threads
Black embroidery floss

■ **1.** This quilt requires 12 nine-patch blocks. The blocks are constructed with strip piecing. Cut one 2½″ × 44″ strip from each of your 8 block prints. Cut these crossgrain, perpendicular to the selvage of the fabrics. Cut one 2½″ × 44″ strip from the light background print. The fabrics should be of equal color intensity and look pleasing together regardless of their order. Select 3 of the strips for the first band, and sew these together down their 44″ length using a ¼″ seam allowance. Select 3 more and seam these in the same manner. Seam the remaining 3. Press the bands flat and cut them into 2½″ segments. Select one 3-square segment from each group and assemble the nine patch, sewing the strips together horizontally into blocks. Rearrange the row order for the widest variety. Sew 12 blocks together.

■ **2.** Cut six 6½″ squares from the light background print. Cut 10 setting triangles from the light background using pattern A from the Rainbow Daisy quilt, page 75. Cut 4 corner triangles using template A from the Sailboats quilt, page 23. The quilt top will be arranged with a diagonal set. Sew the first row together by positioning 2 setting triangle A's on either side of a nine patch. The position is illustrated in the photograph. Refer to the lower corner of the quilt interior. The second row is formed by sewing a triangle A to a nine patch/solid square/nine patch/triangle A. Sew the second row to the first row. Sew a corner triangle to the outside edge of the first row. Following the photograph, continue to assemble the diagonal rows, alternating nine patches with solid blocks. Each row will begin with a triangle positioned to maintain the quilt edge. When the rows are completed, press the seams flat.

■ **3.** Transfer the appliqué cat pattern to template material. The cats can be blindstitched with traditional appliqué methods or with a freezer paper appliqué method; refer to the Glossary for more detailed information. Position the cats on the solid squares. Reverse half of the cat bodies, so they face into the quilt. Blindstitch the cats to the background. Remove the background fabric from behind the cat appliqués, maintaining ¼″ seam allowance of the background print.

■ **4.** Cut 1½″ green solid strips for the border. Piece the strips for additional length. Cut this border lengthwise along the gain of the fabric, but piece on the bias to minimize the appearance of the seams. Sew this border to the sides of the quilt first, trim, and add to the top and lower edges.

■ **5.** Cut outside borders, 4″ × 34½″ and two 4″ × 33½″, from the light print. The fabric I selected for this border had a definite up-and-down pattern. In order to maintain the direction of the print, it was necessary to cut the long side borders lengthwise along the grain, and the top and lower borders crossgrain. If this is not a consideration with your print, cut all 4 borders lengthwise on the grain for stability and strength. Press the top after it is assembled.

■ **6.** Layer the top, batting, and backing. Baste the quilt for hand or machine quilting. Quilt around the cats, and add the tail detail with quilting. I superimposed a heart and leaf on the nine-patch blocks for a quilting motif. A traditional tulip design was quilted in the border.

■ **7.** When all the quilting is completed, bind the raw edges with green solid.

■ **8.** Embroider the kitties' smiles with a backstitch, using 1 strand of embroidery floss.

Finished quilt and patterns for this design
are on the next two pages.

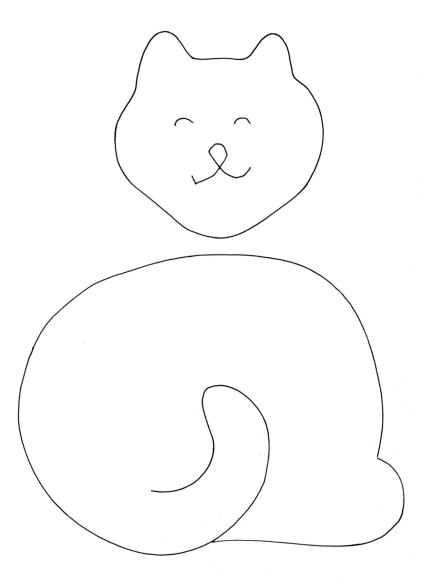

Full-Size Pattern

Seam Allowance Not Included

country hearts and bows

Time Frame 3

Finished size: 33½″ × 42¼″

Materials required

1 yard print for border and binding
1 yard white print or solid background
Assorted pastel scraps for hearts, pieced blocks, and borders
1¼ yards backing
Baby-sized batting
Matching sewing and quilting threads

■ **1.** Enlarge and transfer the Country Hearts quilt pattern, page 51, to template material. This quilt requires 12 blocks using the design. Cut and piece the hearts according to the directions in step 1, page 51. Appliqué the hearts to 6″ squares of the white fabric.

■ **2.** Make templates A, B, and C from the shapes shown in the block diagram; add ¼″ seam allowance. Each block uses 4 white triangle A's, 4 pastel triangle A's, 4 different pastel B's, and 4 white triangle C's. Referring to the block diagram, piece 12 of these blocks.

■ **3.** Alternate 2 heart blocks with 2 pieced blocks to form a row for the quilt. This quilt requires 6 rows. All the hearts should be positioned in a downward direction.

■ **4.** Cut 2 border bands 22½″ × 2½″ and bands 34½″ × 2½″. Sew the border to the top and lower edges first, and complete the attachment to the sides of the quilt.

■ **5.** Using template B, cut approximately 40 pieces from assorted fabrics for the pieced border. The long sides will require 11 segments, and the short sides will need 9. If the pieced row is a bit longer than the quilt side, shorten the length of one of the B units to accommodate the measurement. Position this shortened segment in the center of the pieced border to minimize its appearance. Miter the corners to complete the border attachment. Refer to the Glossary for mitering directions.

■ **6.** For the outer border, cut 2 bands 3½″ × 36½″ and 2 bands 3½″ × 33½″. Cut these bands lengthwise along the grain of the fabric. If necessary, piece the border on the bias to minimize the seam appearance. Attach the long side borders first, and complete the assembly by sewing the borders to the top and lower edges. Press.

■ **7.** Layer the top, batting, and backing. Pin and baste the layers for hand or machine quilting. Quilt around the edge of the hearts. Quilt the pieced blocks following their seams. Quilt "in the ditch" of the border seams. I quilted a small heart motif into the outer border of this quilt.

■ **8.** When the quilting is completed, bind the raw edges.

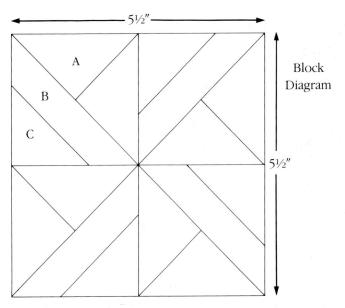

Block Diagram

Enlarge Pattern to Size Indicated

Seam Allowance Not Included

amish love

Time Frame 2

Finished size: 38″ × 48″

Materials required

1¼ yards black solid
1 yard assorted solids, at least 5 colors
1½ yards backing
½ yard teal solid for binding
Baby-sized batting
Matching sewing and quilting threads

■ **1.** Transfer the heart pattern to template material. Construct a four patch of 4 solid fabrics using the 3½″ square pattern from the Eyelet and Lace quilt, page 15. (This measurement includes ¼″ seam allowance.) Sew 4 squares together, 2 rows of 2 squares, using a sewing machine. Press. Position the heart pattern over the four patch and mark the outline on the right side. Cut the heart shape out, adding a scant ¼″ seam allowance, with your scissors. Baste the seam allowance under, even with the marked line, and press. Make 6 pieced hearts for this quilt.

■ **2.** Construct 6 pieced background blocks for the hearts. Cut 1 black 6½″ × 10½″ rectangle per block. Cut 2 black smaller rectangles 2½″ × 6½″. Cut four 2½″ squares from the assorted solids. Sew a square to either side of the 2½″ × 6½″ rectangles. Seam 1 of these units along the 10½″ side of a large rectangle. Repeat this for the opposite side of the large rectangle, creating the block. Refer to block 2 diagram, page 20. Press. Center the heart appliqué on the block and blindstitch.

■ **3.** The alternating pieced blocks are an extended nine patch. The quilt requires 6 of these blocks. Begin by constructing a nine-patch center for the block that has 5 different 2½″ squares of solids and four 2½″ squares of black. Each block has a first and third row with 2 colored squares joined to a black center square. The middle row has 2 black squares joined by a colored square in the center. Sew the 3 rows together. Press. Cut 4 black 2½″ × 6½″ rectangles. Cut 4 different solid 2½″ squares. Seam a black rectangle to the top and lower edges of the nine patch. Sew a square to either side of the 2 black rectangles. Seam these 2 bands to the block sides. This block is the same as block diagram, page 72.

■ **4.** Sew the first row of blocks together: 2 nine-patch blocks joined by a heart block in the center. The second row is made of 2 heart blocks with a nine patch in the center. Repeat for 2 more rows. When your 4 rows are complete, sew them together. Press.

■ **5.** Cut 2 black borders 40½″ × 4½″, and 2 borders 30½″ × 4½″. Each corner will need a four patch constructed of four 2½″ assorted solid squares. Sew the long borders to the sides of the quilt. Sew a corner square to either side of the 2 remaining border bands. Seam the completed top and lower bands to the remaining edges of your quilt top. Press.

■ **6.** Layer the quilt, batting, and backing. Pin and baste the quilt for hand or machine quilting.

■ **7.** When the quilting is completed, bind the outside raw edge with a 1½″ teal solid binding strip.

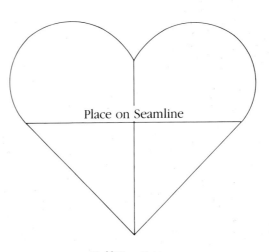

Place on Seamline

Half-Size Pattern

Seam Allowance Not Included

86

lambie pie

Time Frame 3

Finished size: 26″ × 32″

Materials required

¾ yard pink solid for background and pieced border
½ yard yellow print for border
⅛ yard each of green print, yellow gingham, and yellow calico for border flowers
½ yard white for lamb appliqué
⅛ yard black for lamb nose, feet, and ears
Print or solid scraps for collar, bell, and butterfly
1 yard striped print for outer border
1 yard backing
½ yard yellow for binding
Baby-sized batting
Matching sewing and quilting threads

■ **1.** Enlarge lamb to sizes indicated with copy machine. Transfer the appliqué pattern for the lamb to the right side of the fabric and cut the fabric with a scant ¼″ seam allowance. Baste the seam allowance under and press.

■ **2.** Cut your pink background fabric 18½″ × 24½″. Position the lamb on the background. The legs should be placed under the body, so the lower body edge overlaps their top edge. The head can overlap the collar and face, eliminating the need to turn this seam allowance under. The ear should be placed over the head. Blindstitch these to the background. Position and blindstitch the butterfly as well. When the appliqués are complete, remove the background from behind them, maintaining ¼″ seam allowance.

■ **3.** Use the enlarged square pattern from the Eyelet and Lace quilt, page 15, to make a template. With it, cut four 3½″ squares of yellow border fabric. (This measurement includes ¼″ seam allowance.) Enlarge and transfer patterns A and B to template material. Cut 28 A's from the yellow print and 28 B's from the pink background fabric. Crease the A and B shapes to find the centerline along their curved edges. Mark this crease with a pin. It will be necessary to clip into the concave curve of shape A at intervals of approximately ¼″, up to but not beyond the seamline. Pin the two at the center crease, and at the outside edges. Keep the pins perpendicular to the outer edge and bring the raw edges together. Hand-stitch along the seamline. To machine-stitch this curve, set your machine length at 20 stitches per inch. Sew on the stitch line, removing the pins just as you arrive at them. Press the completed units with the seam going toward the larger shape. The side borders will be made of 6 drunkard's path shapes. Sew 2 units to create a scalloped opening. Mark and cut 28 leaves and 14 flowers. Sew the leaf and flower appliqués into this section where B shapes are seamed. The top and lower borders are made of 8 drunkard's path units. Sew a 3½″ square of the yellow print to the outside ends of the top and lower border bands. Sew the side borders to the appliquéd

picture first, and complete the assembly by stitching the top and lower borders.

■ **4.** The final border used on this quilt was cut from a striped fabric. When using a stripe, purchase at least 1 yard. Select a pleasing stripe pattern within the fabric, and cut adding ¼″ beyond the printed outline of the design. Cut 4 striped bands that are the length of the sides plus the width of the striped border. Add an additional ½″ for seam allowance to this measurement. Sew the top and lower bands to the quilt, ending the seam ¼″ from the outside edge. These bands should extend at least the width of this border plus seams. Add the 2 remaining bands to the sides. Refer to the Glossary for instructions on mitering the corners to complete the assembly. Press.

■ **5.** Layer the quilt top, batting, and backing. Baste the quilt for hand or machine quilting. Quilt around the appliqué and echo its outline as a filler for the background. The lamb was quilted with circular swirls to create a feeling of texture. I transferred cookie-cutter shapes of flowers and birds to fill in empty background areas. Quilt around the outer borders ¼″ from the seams to secure this edge.

■ **6.** When the quilting is completed, bind the outer edge.

Patterns for this design are on the next page.

Lambie Pie
(continued)

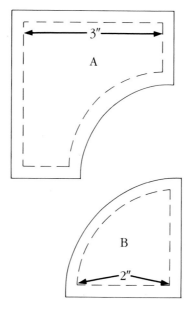

Seam Allowance Included

Enlarge Patterns to Sizes Indicated

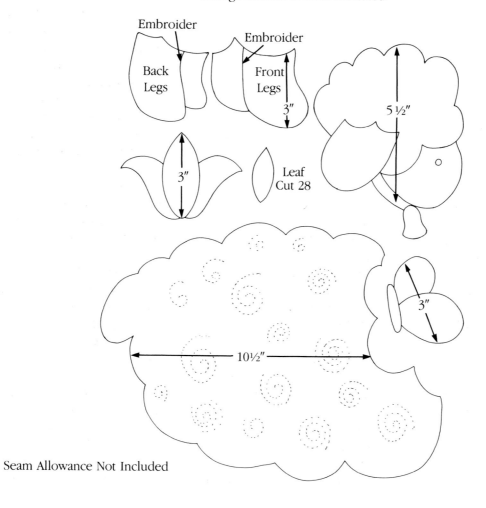

Seam Allowance Not Included

tumbling bears

Time Frame 3

Finished size: 42″ hexagon

Materials required

1 yard light print for background of appliquéd blocks, binding, and border
¼ yard each of 6 coordinating pastel prints
¼ yard beige print for bear appliqués
⅛ yard pink print for bear paw, pad, and inner-ear appliqués
⅛ yard muslin for bear muzzles
1¼ yards backing
Baby-sized batting
Matching sewing and quilting threads

■ **1.** Enlarge and transfer the diamond and the hexagon to template material. Cut 6 hexagons from your background fabric. Cut 6 diamonds from each of the 6 pastel prints.

■ **2.** Enlarge and trace the bear patterns. Position the tracing over a light source. Use a light box, or a sunlit window. A lit television screen will also serve as a light box. Tape the pattern to the glass. Tape the hexagons with the right sides toward you to the glass, over the bear picture. Mark the bear outline on the hexagons for a position guide. Once marked, remove hexagons. Then lay the bear fabric over the light source and trace the appliqués. Remember that you will be adding a scant ¼″ seam allowance beyond the marked line as you cut each section. It will therefore be necessary to reposition the fabric, accommo-

dating the seam allowance, for each body section.

■ **3.** Cut out the appliqué section, adding ¼″ seam allowance. Over the bear pattern remaining on your light source, tape a hexagon on which you have previously traced the bear outline. Align the bear shape. Position the cut-out ears and arms correctly on the hexagon. Baste these to the background ½″ in from their outside edges. Position and baste the head and the body sections. These will overlap the arms and ears. Baste these in place, ½″ inside their cut raw edges. Complete placement of the legs, basting these as well. Blindstitch the appliqué sections, turning the seam allowance under with the needle. With the bear stitched down, add the pink paws, pads, and inner-ear sections. Add a muslin muzzle at this time. Blindstitch these appliqués in place. Cut out the background layers under each appliqué. Trim this background fabric to a ¼″ seam allowance. Mark the facial expression, and embroider these details with a single strand of embroidery floss. The facial features were embroidered with black floss, using a small backstitch. The detail stitching on the body of the bear is a running stitch with a single strand of tan floss.

■ **4.** Repeat this appliqué procedure for the second version of the bear. Two more bear positions are

made by reversing the tracing of each of these bears. The 2 remaining versions will be of your own design. Think of this bear as jointed. Use the same head and arm position, but move the legs for a new design. Make a total of 6 bear hexagons.

■ **5.** Choose 1 diamond from each of your 6 prints. Mark ¼″ seam allowance for accuracy. Sew 3 together to form half of the center star. Repeat this for the additional half. Carefully lay the 2 together, checking centerlines. Sew 1 seam across, joining the 2 halves. Do not sew into your seam allowance on the outside star seams. Refer to photograph.

Sew a hexagon to 2 adjacent outer star edges. Sew from the junction of the star seams out along a hexagon side. Repeat this procedure for the adjoining side. Continue to attach the remaining 5 hexagons. Do not sew into your ¼″ seam allowance. Sew a diamond opposite the point of each of the center star diamonds. Piece this between 2 hexagons. Refer to the photograph as a guide.

■ **6.** Complete the outer star border by sewing 3 diamonds to each hexagonal corner. Sew 1 diamond to 2 hexagon sides, and add the final diamond between these 2. Distribute the colors equally around the quilt top.

■ **7.** Cut 6 outside borders from your light print, 2½″ in width and

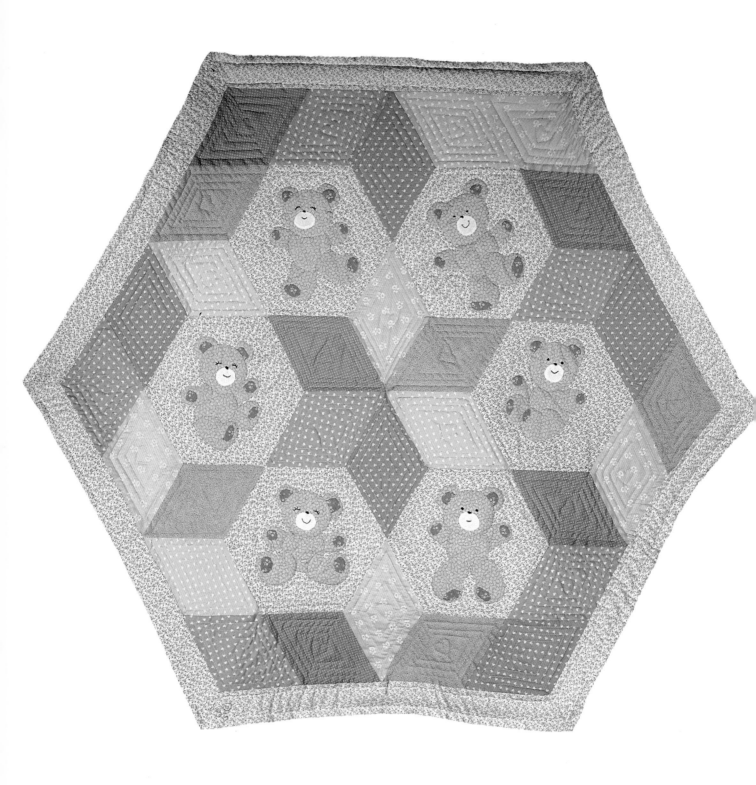

as long as the side of the quilt top, approximately 19½". Adjust the length of this band for your individual quilt edge. The short sides of the bands should be cut off at a 60° angle to the centerline of the corner diamonds. Sew the bands to the quilt top and lower edges, avoiding running into your seam allowance on the outer edges. After attaching the 2 adjoining sides, sew the bands together. Refer to photograph.

■ **8.** Cut your backing and batting about 2" wider than the quilt top. Layer the top, batting, and backing. Pin and baste the layers for hand or machine quilting. Quilt around the appliqués. Quilt at ½" intervals, echoing the shape of each of the diamonds. Quilt the border ¼" around the inner seam.
■ **9.** Bind the raw edges of the quilt with self-binding cut 1½" wide along the lengthwise grain of the light print fabric. After attach-

ing the binding, add an additional quilting line ¼" from the outside edge of the quilt.
■ **10.** Seam a casing across the top edge to insert a rod for hanging. If the quilt does not lie flat on the wall, sew additional casings following the outside shape of the top and upper sides of the quilt. Insert a smaller casing shape cut of mat board into these sleeves to support the outer edges.

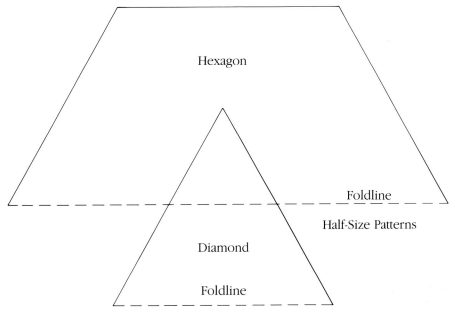

Hexagon

Foldline

Half-Size Patterns

Diamond

Foldline

Seam Allowance Not Included

Half-Size Patterns

Seam Allowance Not Included

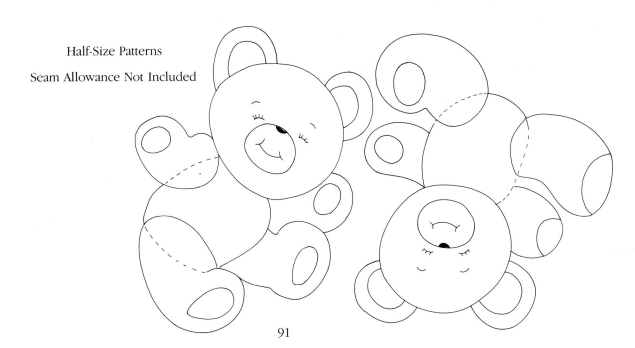

91

n i n e

grace's tulip

Time Frame 3

Finished size: 38″ × 54″

Materials required

1 yard light print for background
1½ yards purple print for border and blocks
½ yard green print for piecing and appliqués
¼ yard pink print for piecing and bud appliqué
¼ yard purple solid for piecing and tulip appliqué
1½ yards backing
½ yard print for binding
Baby-sized batting
Matching sewing and quilting threads

■ **1.** Cut out fifteen 6″ squares from your light background print. This measurement includes seam allowance. Refer to the block diagram. Construct 15 blocks for this quilt. Enlarge and transfer pattern B from the Candy Corn quilt, page 29, to template material. This template is for a 2″ finished triangle, with ¼″ seam allowance included. Each block will use the following B triangles: 8 purple print, 4 pink print, 2 green print, and 2 purple solid. Note that the diagonally opposite corners of the block have the same fabric placement. Begin by piecing 2 corner squares together. Sew the purple print triangles to either side of this square to complete the corner unit. Sew these to all sides of the 6″ background squares.

■ **2.** Sew the blocks into 5 rows that contain 3 blocks. Press.

■ **3.** Mark the appliqué fabrics on the right side using the tulip templates. Cut your appliqués adding a scant ¼″ seam allowance, and blindstitch them to the background squares. The pink bud will be overlapped by the flower, so baste only the top edge under. The stem will also be overlapped by the leaves and flower, so baste only the long sides.

■ **4.** The first border is made of rows of triangles, squares, and rectangles that transform the appearance of the blocks into stars. At each block edge where purple print triangles meet, sew a pair of purple print triangles positioned to create a large triangle shape for the border band. Attach these to light print rectangles cut 2½″ × 4½″. The top and lower edge borders will start with a 2½″ light print square. This is attached to a pair of purple print/light print B triangles, separated by 2½″ × 4½″ light print rectangles. Sew these bands to the top and lower quilt edges. Press. The side borders are constructed as the top and lower bands were, except that they begin and end with a 2½″ green print square. Follow each green print square with a 2½″ light print square. Two pairs of purple print triangles sewn with light print tri-angles on their diagonal will follow, and these pairs will be separated by 2½″ × 4½″ light print rectangles. The sides will require 10 triangles, sewn into 5 paired sections, and 4 rectangles. Sew the side borders to the quilt and press.

■ **5.** Cut a second border from the light print: two 2½″ × 44½″ for the sides and two 2½″ × 32½″ for the top and bottom. Sew the top and lower bands to the quilt, then add the sides to complete.

■ **6.** Cut 2 top and bottom borders 3½″ × 48½″ and 2 side borders 3½″ × 38½″ from the purple print, lengthwise along the grain. Sew the side borders to the quilt, and then the lower and top borders. Press.

■ **7.** Layer the quilt, batting, and backing together. Pin and baste the layers for hand or machine quilting. Quilt around the appliqué sections, and ¼″ around all the patchwork shapes. The border was quilted with a continuous curving twist.

■ **8.** When all the quilting is completed, bind the outside edge with 1½″ binding.

Patterns for this design are on the next page.

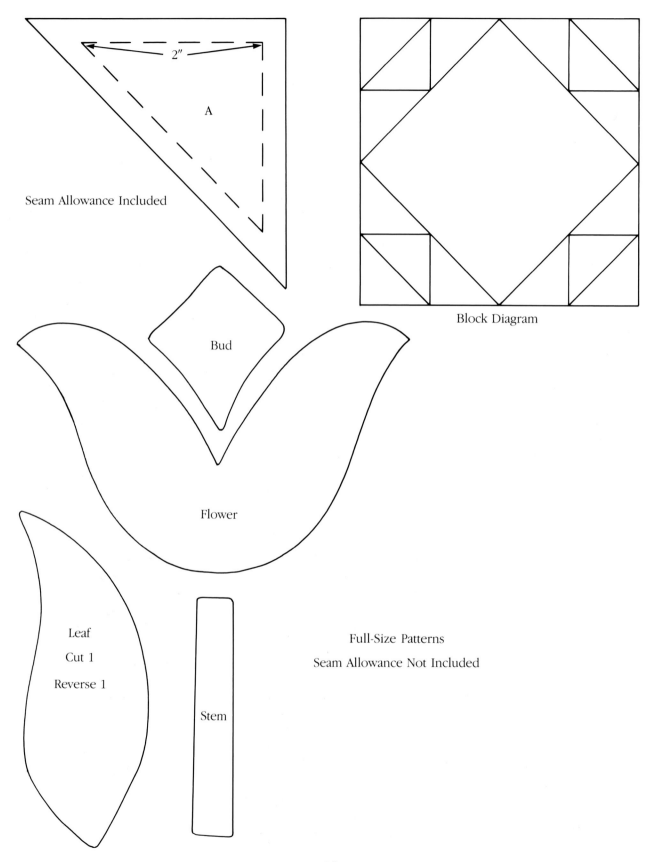

2"

A

Seam Allowance Included

Block Diagram

Bud

Flower

Leaf

Cut 1

Reverse 1

Stem

Full-Size Patterns

Seam Allowance Not Included

mixed blessings

Time Frame 3

• • •

This quilt is a sampler created with patterns and templates from throughout this book. You will need to enlarge patterns as specified on the pages where the patterns appear. The geometric templates are commonly found in traditional patchwork blocks. The shapes will finish to either 2″ or 3″ units. When using assorted patterns, the success of the project depends on fabric selection. Choose and maintain a color scheme. I selected blue, yellow, and pink, and a lesser amount of green. Find a limited number of prints in the colors you plan to use, and repeat them throughout. The materials list for this quilt is provided for your convenience. I do hope that you use it as a guide to design your own quilts.

Finished size: 44″ × 53″

Materials required

1 yard blue print for border
½ yard coordinating yellow print
¼ yard yellow medium-sized print
½ yard yellow solid
¼ yard each of 5 pink prints
½ yard light print for background
1½ yards calico for backing
½ yard yellow print for binding
Baby-sized batting
Matching sewing and quilting threads

■ **1.** The quilt top is divided into 3 vertical rows. Starting on the left side from the top to the lower edge of this row, the patterns used are: pinwheels made from pattern A of the Sailboats quilt, page 23; flying geese made from patterns A and B of the Candy Corn quilt, page 29; 3″ square from the Eyelet and Lace quilt, page 15; heart pattern from the Country Hearts quilt, page 51, appliquéd on a 12½″ × 9½″ white background. These are followed by stars cut from the Twinkling Stars quilt pattern, page 45, appliquéd on a 12½″ × 9½″ yellow background. (The backgrounds and pieced patterns include seam allowance.) The row is finished with a variable star made from patterns A and B of the Nine Patch and Stars quilt, page 26.

■ **2.** The middle vertical row of this quilt begins with 3 print triangles and 3 strip-pieced triangles using pattern B from the Pinwheel Scraps quilt, page 32. The balloons are taken from the Little Bear's Sunny Day quilt, page 57, and are appliquéd to a 12½″ × 15½″ light print background (includes seam allowance). Two pinwheel blocks follow, constructed as in the first vertical row. Three 3½″ × 12½″ bands are pieced underneath the pinwheels. The final design for this row uses the block pattern from the Rainbow Daisy quilt, page 75, in the center of which a bunny from the Sweet Baby Quilt, page 59, is appliquéd.

■ **3.** The third row, on the right side of the quilt, begins with a 12″ pieced star made from patterns A, B, and C from the Pieced Stars quilt, page 38. I followed this with the engine pattern from the Little Sleepy Railroad quilt, page 53, appliquéd to a yellow background cut 12½″ × 9½″ (including seam allowance). This is followed by 6 flying geese made as in the first row. Two rows of four 3″ squares from the Eyelet and Lace quilt, page 15, are sewn underneath the flying geese. A sailboat block from the Sailboats quilt, page 23, was assembled and attached below the squares. This row was completed with 4 drunkard's path units made from patterns A and B given in the Lambie Pie quilt, page 88.

■ **4.** For the border cut two 4½″ × 45½″ strips lengthwise and two 4½″ × 36½″ strips also lengthwise. Sew the 2 long strips to the quilt sides first, and then complete the assembly by seaming the top and lower borders to the quilt. Press.

■ **5.** Layer the quilt top, backing, and batting. Pin and baste the layers for hand or machine quilting. Quilt "in the ditch" around the patchwork designs and around the appliqués. Accent empty areas with decorative quilting motifs. Use cookie cutters and traditional quilting designs for inspiration.

■ **6.** When the quilting is completed, bind the edges with 1½″ yellow print binding.

Finished quilt for this design is shown on the next page.